THE CENTURY SPEAKS
MERSEY
voices

Gerry Lipson (centre) at RAF station Wahn, outside Cologne, during National Service days, 1949.

THE
CENTURY
SPEAKS

MERSEY
voices

*Memories of Merseyside people
compiled by Diana Pulson from interviews by Ev Draper
for the* **BBC Radio Merseyside** *series*
The Century Speaks

TEMPUS

First published 1999
Reprinted 2004
Copyright © BBC Radio Merseyside, 1999

Tempus Publishing Limited
The Mill, Brimscombe Port,
Stroud, Gloucestershire, GL5 2QG

ISBN 0 7524 1835 1

Typesetting and origination by
Tempus Publishing Limited
Printed in Great Britain

The Dock Road and Overhead Railway, 1929.

CONTENTS

Foreword		6
Introduction		7
Acknowledgements		8
1.	Looking back	9
2.	Getting by	31
3.	Work and play	49
4.	Life and death	77
5.	Beliefs, fears, justice and injustice	93
6.	Food and drink	109
7.	Into the new millennium	119

Mick Ord

FOREWORD

Since BBC Radio Merseyside began in 1967 thousands of people have appeared on our airwaves. The list of interviewees reads like a 'Who's Who' of British life since the Second World War – The Beatles, numerous Prime Ministers, politicians of all hues, and sporting superstars, many of whom now have their place in the history books.

But we should not just rely on the words of the rich and famous. History in the twentieth century is much more about ordinary people than Kings and Queens.

What better place to hear the voices of real people than on your local BBC radio station? What better place to read about them, than in this marvellous chronicle of local life which Diana Pulson has edited?

The Merseyside and Cheshire area is rich in history and I believe that it is to books like this that future generations will turn to find out what life was really like over the past 100 years.

It is easy to look at the past with rose-tinted glasses but this is not an exercise in nostalgia: These are real lives, as one of the interviewees Lena Prince explains: 'On Empire day we danced around the Maypole. We'd be singing *Rule Brittania* – I didn't know what it meant but it was very grand. It mentioned a charter and us never going to be slaves. I did not have a clue what it was all about.'

As well as the rich memories in words, I hope you will also enjoy the wonderful photographs that Diana has collected, many of which have never been published before. The combination of the words and pictures mean that by the end of the book, the century has really spoken to you.

Mick Ord
Managing Editor BBC Radio Merseyside

Diana Pulson   Ev Draper

INTRODUCTION

People of all ages talking about their lives…what better way to capture the spirit of the century? That's why the BBC – in conjunction with the British Library – embarked on the largest oral history project ever undertaken in Europe. An oral history producer was appointed in every part of the country and Ev Draper, from BBC Radio Merseyside, listened to more than 150 local men and women, as they remembered the highs and lows of their lives, as well as how the community has changed, over the last 100 years. My role in all this has been much simpler – to act as something of a foot soldier; listening to some of the interviews and then compiling these wonderful memories into a book.

It has been a fascinating, humbling experience because though as a Liverpudlian myself, I knew all about the good times and the bad times our city has known, to actually listen to people talking about them, added a new dimension. This, of course, is where oral history excels. When you hear the quavering tones of 105-year-old William Goddard telling how he was in chapel in Widnes when the Relief of Mafeking was announced from the pulpit, history not only leaps to life, but the hair stands up on the back of your neck. Centenarian William Goddard however, is only the start of the story of Merseyside during the twentieth century. Apart from the great set-piece dramas of two World Wars, the city and its folk have been through so much – and still come out smiling.

The abject poverty in which so many people lived for so long in the 1920s and 1930s makes you flinch. Five and six in a bed, not enough to eat, bugs running up and down the bedposts, real slum conditions. How on earth did they put up with it and survive? Yet they did. They pawned their clothes on a Monday to be able to eat during the week, then somehow managed to scrape enough money together to take them out for the weekend. At the opposite end of the scale there were the wealthy families some of whom adopted a hedonistic attitude and had no idea of how the other half lived, but there were also the philanthropists from well known families like the Rathbones, the Bibbys, and the Holts who possessed the same social conscience as their forebears and knew their duty to society.

It is, though, the ordinary people who tug at your heartstrings and, as for the working class womenfolk of Merseyside, they emerge as positive Bodiceas, in their determination to keep their families going. They worked day and night to make ends meet, took in washing and ironing, sold fruit and veg from handcarts. Anything to earn a few bob. Thankfully, as we reach the Millennium, those days have by and large gone. The Welfare State has seen to that and a good thing it is too. However there are still people enduring hard times as well as unpleasant aspects of society.

One of my tasks has been to persuade people to lend me their precious photographs to illustrate this book, which has meant that while they dug them out of the drawers and attics, I have been a guest in their homes. Many hailed from humble beginnings, but what pride they take in their neatly run houses, their well tended gardens, the fact that pictures of grandchildren who are university graduates stand on the sideboard, though they themselves often had little or no education.

Ev's interviews – as you will see as you read on – reveal aspects of old Liverpool which were not particularly pleasant. The enmity between Catholics and Protestants which manifested itself so violently on 12 July, the day the Orange Lodge marched. Then there was the dominance of the Catholic Church itself when the priests' word was law and every Catholic home, no matter how poor, was expected to give financial support each week. The indignity of a Catholic marrying a Protestant being denied a ceremony in front of the main altar. Sometimes it took place in the vestry. Again these times have passed. Looking back on life generally, you realise that what some will always think of as 'the good old days' were no such thing. But life was not all gloom. There was the same Scouse cheerfulness which persists to this day; a make-the-most-of-it attitude which was obviously as integral to the Liverpool character at the beginning of the century as it is at the end. Of course the city has changed dramatically in 100 years. The docks are a shadow of their former selves, sadly the famous Overhead Railway is no more, Coopers with its wonderful smell of roasting coffee beans is a distant memory and posh Bold Street, once considered the local Bond Street, is today just an ordinary thoroughfare. Politically the city has been through a few traumas. Yet despite everything Liverpool, warts and all, soldiers on.

It has not been possible for me to listen to all the 150 interviews Evelyn conducted for this important social survey, so the anecdotes, views and information I have selected show only a fragment of how Merseyside folk have lived and survived during the twentieth century. They are though, I hope, representative. I do hope you enjoy them.

Diana Pulson

ACKNOWLEDGEMENTS

My thanks to all the people who took the trouble to search through their family albums to provide illustrations for this book, and to the *Liverpool Daily Post* and *Echo*, for giving permission for the use of photographs from their archives. Also to Lizzie Meachim, researcher on *The Century Speaks*.

CHAPTER 1
Looking back

William Goddard in 1914, with a group of friends, many of whom were to die in the war. William, on the back row, extreme right, would have been nineteen at the time of the photograph.

New Century

When the twentieth century arrived in 1900 the streets were dressed up as they had been for the end of the Boer War. There were all sorts of celebrations. I was six at the time and lived in Widnes where I was born and stayed all my life.

We were in chapel when the Relief of Mafeking was announced from the pulpit. They let us out. I always felt that the Boer War broke Queen Victoria's heart.

As little boys we wore petticoats – everyone did. Later I wore clogs. I went to school at two and half and there was a big rocking horse which I wanted to ride. But I never got the chance. In the 1914-18 war half of my class got killed.

William Goddard, born 1894

Pride

Whit Monday used to be British Empire Day. It was a big thing then. Mother took the pony and cart and opened up a shop en route, selling apples, pears and coconuts. We were very proud of being British and sang patriotic songs. It was the British Empire in its heyday.

Harry Mooney, born 1919

Queen Victoria

When Queen Victoria died in 1901, people wore black armbands. I was three at the time and I can remember seeing children coming out of school with them on. It was the heyday of the British Empire. My mother had a picture of Queen Victoria.

We lived in the Dock Master's House at the Albert Dock. My father was the Dock Master. It was a beautiful house, very large with seven bedrooms and seven cellars. The lounge was so big you could dance two sets of Lancers in it. Mother had to have help in the house, because there was too much for her to do.

There were so many ships in the Mersey that you could hardly put a pin between them, ranging from barges to liners. There were even a few sailing ships. The docks were my playground. By the time I was seven I could climb a rigging like nobody's business, though I was forbidden to do so. They called me Madge Madcap.

If a liner was docking at the stage, others boats had to wait. The ferry was held up. There was a station at the Pier Head, so that those disembarking from the liners could step straight onto a train. You would see horse-drawn carriages waiting for the tide so that they could use the floating landing stage.

A familiar sound was the Bootle Cow – the foghorn at Seaforth which made a sound like a cow.

Madge Parry, born 1899

Dockland In Its Heyday

Liverpool docks in their prime were a tremendous sight. They stretched for ten or twelve miles, which you could see if you took the Overhead Railway and had a day out. Over 15,000 men worked there. There were markets where the women had jobs. Firms like Tate and Lyle. They were great days.

It was a matriarchal society. Granny was the boss. You'd have three generations in one tenement. Men had no say in the house, but spoke very loud in the pubs. Drink, of course, was the curse: there was nothing else to do, no clubs or cinemas. So it was into the pub. There were pubs every ten yards around the docks and when people were under the influence, plenty of squabbles and fights.

The priest could do what he liked. If there was a fight the police kept out of it.

Father Denis McDonnell, born 1907

Runcorn Transporter

When the Runcorn Transporter Bridge was built in 1905, it swayed in the wind. The day it opened we all had a day off.

William Goddard, born 1894

Smells

The docks had various smells. You could smell brandy going into Harrison's warehouse at the Albert Dock. Everything came in, including rubber from South America. Once they brought a ship, which had been used to take prisoners to Australia, into Salthouse Dock. It was terrible the conditions in which the prisoners had been kept.

When you were in a hansom cab, the

Agnes Maddison and friend in New Brighton, 1947.

horses had difficulty negotiating the cobbles along the Dock Road. There was only room for two in the cabs and I can remember being squashed in between my mother and father when returning home from an organ recital in St George's Hall.

Liverpool was a wonderful place. During the May Day parades in Princes Park, men with fish nets drove by in big lorries and you put money in as they passed.

The Palm House in Sefton Park was crammed with flowers. The perfume was almost overpowering.

Madge Parry, born 1899

Three-year-old Vera Jeffers seen with her aunt Vi, in Trouville Road.

Scottie Road

My mother had eight children but two died. Little Willie was run over by a handcart when he was three and George died of whooping cough.

Scotland Road, where I was born, was known throughout the world. Great Homer Street was always lit up. During the Second World War, when bombs dropped around Scotland Road, some bodies were not found. My dad was an undertaker and they filled coffins with sand rather than upset families of people missing. I never forgot Scotland Road.

Agnes Maddison, born 1927

Hitler

Liverpool was badly hit during the war but it was never published. They did not want Hitler to realise how much damage he had done.

Vera Jeffers, born 1925

Trams

There were first and second class seats on trams. One woman who was drunk was sitting downstairs on a tram when she should have been upstairs. When challenged she said 'It's my birthday. I thought I'd give my arse a treat.'

Father Denis McDonnell, born 1907

Struggling

Scotland Road was a marvellous place to live, even if everyone was struggling. The bobbies were very good in those days. If they saw you swinging on lamp-posts or doing something you shouldn't they would give you a kick up the backside and send you on your way. Or they would take you to your mum and say 'Don't let him out again.' It did none of us any harm.

In 1929 there were the knockers-up, especially important for the dockers who had to be up early. They had long poles and used to knock on windows.

Everything was horse drawn and the only way to cross the Mersey was on the ferry. It was a terrible thing when they took down the Overhead Railway. Today it would have made a lot of money for the council.

George Armstrong, born 1929

Princes Boulevard

Princes Boulevard in Liverpool 8 was very posh, when I was young. We used to play rounders in Princes Park after school. They were grand times. We never had a holiday but we would go to Seacombe and walk to New Brighton. It cost a penny to cross the Mersey.

Lena Prince, born 1923

The Mersey Tunnel

When the first Mersey Tunnel was opened in 1934 there were children singing on the steps of St

Public reminder not to talk too much.

George's Hall. They were dressed as flowers and my sister was a daisy. The tunnel was opened by the King and Queen, George V and Queen Mary. I remember getting a medal.

Lena Prince, born 1923

Victorian Houses

Where the Royal Hospital stands now there used to be a mass of little Victorian houses. They had railings and cellars. Grandfather lived in one street; grandmother in the next street but two. There was family all round. My dad worked for a haulage contractor. He used to go to Smithdown Place to see the horses all dressed for the May Day procession. The men wore flat caps and hob-nailed boots.

Ann Roberts, born 1937

The Bond Street Of The North

Bold Street used to be very expensive and posh, like Bond Street in London. When I left school, I went to work with my auntie May at a shop there called Margaret, Countess of Mayo. There was a real Countess of Mayo who, I believe, was paid for lending her name to the shop. I never saw her. It was a beautiful place. They sold ladies lingerie, handbags, gloves, blouses, knitwear, hosiery: everything was very expensive. Kid gloves cost £10 a pair, you'd pay £20 for a brooch even though it was costume jewellery. You had to call every customer 'Madam' and there was a chair at each counter for 'Madam'. 'Madam' always sat down.

My job at first was to go for stamps and make the tea; run and get the girls' lunch. Wages were not high but you got 3d for every £1 you took. Then I got a job doing the ironing, three storeys up in the attic. There was no heating and I had chilblains on my hands and up the back of my legs. You ironed on a table with a blanket on it. Sometimes I'd iron the blanket and wrap it round me for warmth. Then I became a window dresser.

One day an elderly lady with a lorgnette came in. She looked like Queen Mary and asked to see some blouses. Another who had a note for £15 for something she had brought back, could not find anything she wanted and gave it to me. I bought a blouse and cami-knicks and felt the whole cheese.

I was only earning 17s 6d a week. It went up to £1 but the war came and I was called up and went to work in factory. There I was earning £42 a week – a huge amount. In the factory you wore a cap and tucked your hair in. If it got caught in the machine you would be scalped.

Vera Jeffers, born 1925

Inside the Bold Street shop, Margaret, Countess of Mayo.

Modelling

The shops in Bold Street were very grand with commissioners outside the door. If it was raining, they would shelter you with an umbrella. The dress shops employed mannequins to model clothes as women were shopping and my mother paid £10 – a lot of money in those days – for me to train as a model, when I left school at fifteen. I was 5ft 10 inches tall.
They said they would teach me deportment, but I told them I had learned that at school, from the gym mistress. There was not much training. I was used to carry messages and when I was asked to go and pick up a parcel at the station, I left. My sister was a model at the Bon Marche which was where Lees is now.

Madge Parry, born 1899

The Abdication

The Abdication in 1937, was a terrible shock to my family who were very pro-royal.

We in this country were the last to know about him and Mrs Simpson. People in America knew all about it long before we did. Liverpool people, like everyone, loved the Prince of Wales, but thought Mrs Simpson was dreadful. Later, when he was the Duke of Windsor, I sang in front of him. He was as drunk as a lord.

Joan Wynn-Williams, born 1910

Home Guard

During the war there was the black out and drawn curtains. Father was in the Home Guard. Some of the things he did were just like those you see in *Dad's Army*. As a little lad I took part in exercises, put out imaginary incendiary bombs.

We did not have a television until the 1960s but we listened to the wireless: Itma, Dick Barton, Rob Wilton, Arthur Askey. We also listened to the news reports. I can still remember Winston Churchill's speeches and Neville Chamberlain's the day war broke out. Mum and dad had gone to a later mass than me and, when they came in, they said the priest had announced it. Most of the local men were miners. They were in reserved occupations.

John Griffin, born 1931

Evacuees

There were a lot of children evacuated from Merseyside during the Second World War. I went away at the age of one and ended up in a convent in Criccieth, separated from my brothers and sisters. I remember the beeswax smell of the convent even now. My dad was in the Royal Navy and my mother worked in a munitions factory.

One of the first memories of my dad was when he came to take me home for Christmas in 1945. He had a hanky over his face because he could not cope with the emotion of not having seen us for so long.

A legacy of my evacuation was that

Barbara Phythian (extreme left) applauds Louis Armstrong at a concert at Liverpool Stadium, in the 1950s.

when I came home I had a Welsh accent, for which I was bullied when I went to school in Liverpool.

John McEwan, born 1939

Homesick

There was tremendous homesickness among children who were evacuated during the war. We went to Flint in North Wales but one boy was so miserable, that he skated home all the way to Liverpool.

Barbara Phythian, born 1929

May Blitz

During the May Blitz in 1940, a landmine landed in the centre of Everton Valley and there was a crater which was forty feet deep and just as wide. Tramlines stood up in the air and the Overhead Railway line was down on the ground. The fronts of houses were bashed in. It was a terrible thing.

Harry Mooney, born 1919

Peacocks

Believe it or not, there were once peacocks in Otterspool Park. You would see them if you went to the wartime shows which Cranes Theatre put on. The peacocks were wandering around and there was a little gallery with a band playing.

Barbara Phythian, born 1929

Peace

There were tremendous celebrations when the war ended in 1945. We lived in Liverpool 8 and I can remember my mother running upstairs and saying 'Get up! The war's over.' That night there was a party in the street. Someone had lit a bonfire and we had coats over our nighties. Everyone brought a table, jelly, cakes and banana splits. They made an effigy of Hitler with a coat and trousers and hung him out of the window; then put him on the bonfire. To this day when I see a banana split. I think of that night.

Mary Jenkins, born 1940

Coming Home

Coming out of Lime Street Station with my kit bag on my shoulder at the end of the war in 1945 it was dreadful to see all the devastation. Lewis's had been bombed, St Lukes church.

Jack Lindo, born 1919

Waiting For A Home

After the war, you could be on the Corporation list waiting for a council house for ten years.

Agnes Maddison, born 1927

Sad Days At The Docks

It was criminal what they did to the docks. My dad was on the docks. He'd go out and come back. We were glad to see him back because it would mean he would light a fire and make toast. But it also meant he had not got work. If you did not get picked, you did not get work. If it was raining, he'd come in soaked, and his clothes had to be dried because he had to wear them next day to go back to the docks.

Mary Jenkins, born 1940

Empire Day

On Empire Day we danced round the Maypole. The boys would wear smocks with red kerchiefs; the girls pretty dresses, as they plaited the ribbons of the Maypole. We'd be singing *Rule Brittania*. I did not know what it meant, but it was very grand. It mentioned a charter and us never going to be slaves. I did not have a clue what it was all about.

Lena Prince, born 1923

Girls' day out in London in 1956. Lena Prince is on the left.

Betting

In the days when betting was illegal, there were bookies runners at street corners, People slipped them the money to take to the bookie. There was also pitch and toss. The look-out would give you a shout if they saw the police coming.

Jack Lindo, born 1919

New Brighton

New Brighton was full of B and Bs in the '50s. We were amused by visitors with Yorkshire accents and described them in knitting terms. We spoke plain and they spoke purl. There were a lot of people who came from Scotland to holiday there. One little boy kept shouting 'There's the sea; there's the sea.' Obviously he had never seen it before. Hardly anyone had a car. The visitors arrived by coach and train.

Victoria Street, was full of cafés. Everyone seemed to be eating egg and chips or fish and chips. My mother got me a job in a café when I was fourteen, but after one family walked out without paying, they did not want to know me. She also volunteered me for doing other peoples' shopping. I got paid half a crown for it.

We used to go the beach and paddle and once a year children were allowed into the fairground free.

Diana Dawson, born 1939

Coal

My mother was a Lancashire pit brow lass; she worked in part of the colliery above ground, sorting coal into grades. It was a dirty, cold job. The pit brow lasses went out in the 1920s.

John Griffin, born 1931

Chinese Laundries

There used to be a lot of Chinese laundries in Liverpool. My husband bought one in Park Road. We had a big boiler and tub. My husband did all the stiff collars on a machine. There was a machine for shirts. Sometimes we were up all night. We went to the Chinese church in Sidney Place.

Elizabeth Li, born 1912

The Seaforth entrance to the Overhead Railway, 1910.

Street Parties

The Festival of Britain in 1951 was a big occasion. There were all sorts of street parties. For the Coronation in 1953 we went down the road to the only family we knew who had television. The Coronation was wonderful.

Lena Prince, born 1923

The Overhead Railway

The Overhead Railway was always known as the Dockers' Umbrella. It was the first electric overhead railway in the world and part of Liverpool's history so, when I went to work there, I was very proud. It was 1937 and I was fifteen. At the interview I was asked if I went to church. I said I attended Sunday school. I got a job as a carriage cleaner and worked my way up to inspector.

The Overhead Railway was over seven miles long and there were seventeen stations: Dingle, Herculanean, Toxteth, Brunswick, Wapping, Canning (which was the Custom House), James Street, Pier Head, Princes, Clarence, Nelson, Huskisson, Canada, Brocklebank, Alexander, Seaforth and Litherland on the Southport line at peak periods. The First Class carriages had lino on the floor and plush seats, the Third Class wooden slatted seats. First Class was used by the office people; Third Class by the dockers. There was a lift which took eight. It was used by all the toffee-nosed people. You never got a docker in it.

If you took a round trip you could see all the docks and ships. It was a very happy railway. I suppose it was about thirty feet high. The Overheard ran right through the war, though it was bombed seventeen times. When it was realised that it would cost £2m to repair, the Dock Board closed it down in 1956.

On the last day – Sunday – I was at Seaforth Station and sold the last ticket. I was on the last train from Seaforth to Dingle. It was very sad. People in the city were upset. The Overhead had always been there. I can still remember the noise of the trains.

Stan Soudet, born 1922

Liverpool At Night

If you had been out at night you could walk through Chinatown, without any fear. When we got to the Overhead Railway, on our way back to the Albert Dock, my friend and I walked along beneath it. It was very sad because you saw men sleeping there, covered in newspapers.

Madge Parry, born 1899

Community Spirit

One day about 1947, a leaflet came through the front door announcing a meeting at St Barnabas in Penny Lane, to form a Community Association. We did not know what that meant really. We talked about our neighbours but had no idea what a Community Association was. There

William Wickham, acting Chief Justice inspecting a guard of honour in Aden in 1959.

were hundreds of people there. Men had come back from the forces, others had come together through air-raid duty and allotments. Women had done hospital work, during the war. There was a new spirit of co-operation about; to care for our neighbours.

We wanted to make the peace more valuable and thought that housewives needed some sort of activity, not just looking after babies. Now there are thousands of Community Associations up and down the country.

Jane Saxby, born 1904

Liverpool Re-visited

When I came back to Britain in 1963, after ten years with the Colonial Service, the horses had gone, the trams had gone and the Overhead Railway had gone. This was a great disappointment because I was unable to take my children on it.

William Wickham, born 1926

All Lit Up

As a child, one of the best things was waiting for the lamplighter. We used to cheer when he lit the lamps. It must have been morning before he finished. Then he had to come back and put them out again.

Doris Windsor, born 1917

Shanks

In the world of football, Bill Shankly was a one-off. He asked me to be a scout for Liverpool FC and told me that if I found one good player in ten years, I would be doing well. I said I hoped to do better than that, but he was right. It was very hard to find the standard of player Shankly wanted. He never took rubbish. He did not have a big office, Just a small table, one chair which was his, and two others.

Harry Mooney, born 1919

The Toxteth Riots

After the riots in 1981, Michael Heseltine became Minister for Merseyside. I do not agree with his views but he did a good job for Liverpool. He was for Merseyside. The Task Force did a great job.

Tony McGann, born 1937

Looting

There was a lot of looting in Park Road and Lodge Lane, following the Toxteth Riots. They were coming in taxis to take things. It seemed strange that they brought in a firm from Manchester to do the repairs.

Charles Jenkins, born 1937

Pope's Visit

When the Pope came to Liverpool in 1982 I had a marvellous place in the Anglican Cathedral, just inside the West Door. I could have touched him. We were all clapping and cheering.

But the Orange Lodge was still very militant. I was ashamed when Robert Runcie, the Archbishop of Canterbury came to Liverpool parish church and a member of the Lodge stood up with his banner, when he began to preach. The Archbishop did not retaliate. He knelt at the altar. I felt it was astonishing.

Lena Prince, born 1923

So Much To See

In 1984, we had the Garden Festival. I loved it. There was so much to see; the Japanese Garden, having a ride on the little train. It was on the site of the

Jack Lindo, aged twenty.

Cast Iron Shore where we would sometimes go as children and swim in the Mersey. In those days my brother used to camp there. He'd take a coarse apron of my mother's and two poles. That was his tent.

Lena Prince, born 1923

'Court' Life

When we lived in Herculanean Court in Grafton Street, in the Toxteth area, where I was born, it was on the actual site of the Herculean Pottery Company which is now extinct. There were no black families when I came home from the war. Slowly we got a few Indians and Pakistanis. They seemed to settle in Mulgrave Street and started arriving about 1948-49. They were brought over to do the menial jobs our men refused to do. They went on trains and things like that. Slowly the numbers built up over fifty-odd years. It is sad the reputation the area has because the first people who came were very nice. But their offspring could not find work, so it was a case of idle hands. Then the dope and the drugs came in, though I have not seen any evidence myself.

Jack Lindo, born 1919

Mixed Race

My mother was white and my father black, of mixed race. In the '40s we lived in Rodney Street. There were not many problems but a few pubs where my dad could not go into the lounge.

Once I bought a ticket in Lewis's for 2s 9d to go dancing at the Grafton. I got out of the taxi – big time: but the fellow on the door said I could not go in. I felt terrible but there was nothing you could do. It was the '50s. I did not feel different. When I went to Chester with some mates I was not allowed to go on a boat on the river. I never thought of it being because of my colour. I thought it might be because I came from Liverpool. One of the lads who lived in Everton had a snooker table. When I went there with some pals, I had to sit on the steps. Again, I did not realise it was because of my colour.

Charles Jenkins, born 1937

Thriving

Park Road used to be a thriving area. In the '50s there was a bespoke tailor on the corner, a fresh fish shop. Everything you could think of was in walking distance. You saw few black faces or Oriental children. If you went into Granby Street which was just that bit further away, it was like a foreign country to us. We thought of it as the black area.

Susan Grainger, born 1948

Prejudice

Whether my children had colour problems or not, I do not know. They are all quite light. You would not know they were coloured. The modern terminology – Afro-Carribbean or black

– is right. They used to say 'He's half caste, or quarter caste, or three-quarter caste. Black is an easier word. People know where they stand.

Charles Jenkins, born 1937

The Toxteth Riots

We were living near Lodge Lane when the riots took place in 1981. The police used to come in coaches and park in Grove Park and wait until the call came to go and see to the riots. They were mostly in Granby Street and Upper Parliament Street and were very bad at times. There was looting going on in Lodge Lane. The Rialto, which was a lovely place got burned down. My sister lived in one of the streets off Granby Street and she was really frightened for her life. She was crying her eyes out. There was fighting going on; bottles being thrown, petrol bombs and so forth.

Jack Lindo, born 1919

Posters, advertising a Louis Armstrong concert, decorate a window at Cranes Theatre, in the 1950s.

Tony McGann says farewell to the Prince of Wales after his visit to the Eldonian Village in 1989.

Cranes Theatre

Cranes was a musical landmark in Liverpool, not just a theatre but an emporium, which sold musical instruments, sheet music and records. When I started work there at fifteen, I earned £1 a week. You were apprenticed and learned violin stringing. I was tested on classical music when I applied for the job and I was thrilled to get it. Because of the space they needed, pianos had a floor of their own. There was a lovely little information desk with a love seat in green velvet for customers.

All the stars who were appearing locally came in. Beryl Bainbridge was at the Playhouse; so was Tony Booth. In those days the Empire Theatre did a show called the *Night of One Hundred Stars* and John Mills came in looking for a record of *The Three Juvenile Delinquents*. He was singing it with Laurence Olivier and someone else. Howard Keel wanted to refresh his memory about the songs from *Oklahoma*. A lovely man.

Then as far as records were concerned, we were dealing with 78s, which you put on a wind-up gramophone for them to listen to. Cranes built their own pianos, in the basement, and there are probably some still knocking around. People bought them on the never-never. Children used to learn the piano more then. There were lunchtime concerts where, for 1s you could take your sandwiches and listen to singers like Kathleen Ferrier. And there was ballroom dancing to the latest Victor Sylvester record. Sir Malcolm Sergeant was at the Phil. They were the glory years.

Barbara Phythian, born 1929

The Eldonian Triumph

There were ten of us in two rooms in the council flat in Gildard Gardens where I was born and lived until 1968. It was a slum – the only way to improve things was to bring them down. But the community spirit was brilliant. People did not have much but what they had they shared.

In 1978, the city council were going to demolish the tenement blocks of Eldon and Burlington Street which meant that long-standing communities would be broken up. We'd seen this happen before, when to make way for the new Mersey Tunnel people were sent to Skelmersdale and Kirkby and the outback. A survey showed that ninety-eight per cent of people wanted to stay in the Eldon and Burlington Street area and, as a result, the Eldonians – as we had taken to calling ourselves – completed their first housing scheme, the Portland Gardens Co-operative. Tenement blocks were refurbished into 100 two-storey houses and sheltered housing units. A new era in community-based regeneration had begun.

When a councillor came and said we could stay where we were in the inner city if we included a Housing Co-operative, we did not know what that meant, but we said we would. In fact a Housing Co-operative is like a club. Everyone over the age of eighteen takes a share and you elect a board. A committee is responsible for the everyday management of the site, repairs and collecting rents.112 families agreed to become a Housing Co-operative and round about 1970 we began calling ourselves the Eldonian Village after Eldon Street.

The Prince of Wales visited us on his way to Anfield in the aftermath of the Hillsborough tragedy, and he asked me if anyone had spoken to me about going to have dinner with Margaret Thatcher. He said I would be going – and I did. We were taken into the Cabinet Room where they make all the decisions. They were calling us entrepreneurs. The Prince of Wales had organised it; no doubt about that. I sat by her and she said 'You know Mr McGann, two days ago Ronald Reagan was sitting there.' There were about six of us and she started to talk about small businesses. She said she ran a Christmas Club in Grantham, then she took me over to the window and pointed out the Guards who were on duty.

I walked out, scratching my head as to what it was all about. But eventually we got another fourteen million pounds made available to us. Later Mrs Thatcher visited us but I could not tell anyone in advance for security reasons. I expect people hated me, when she walked through the door, because of what she stood for but, if you want help, as we did, you have to work with the people in power.

Tony McGann, born 1937

Prime Minister Margaret Thatcher, pays a surprise visit to the Eldonian Village and is shown round by Tony McGann, 1989.

Labour Council

In 1983 we were delighted to get a Labour Council, only it was not Labour, it was Militant. All hell broke out in the city; people were made redundant and they went for an illegal budget. Under Derek Hatton, Tony Byrne and Tony Mulhearn, we became known as Toytown and it was a nightmare because they thought a Housing Co-operative was elitist.

We recognised that this was not the national Labour Party. They were a dictatorship. I would have appreciated them more if they had sailed under their own flag and not a flag of convenience. My own personal view was that Militant thought a revolution would start here in Liverpool. They were using the weakest area to get at the government. But whether you like it or not, whether you are Conservative; Labour or Liberal you can only turn a government out through the ballot box. Otherwise you have anarchy.

Tony McGann, born 1937

Shops

Liverpool had wonderful shops. I particularly liked the row opposite the old Boots, where Clayton Square is now. There were some posh places – Bagshaws and the Bon Marche, which is where the Church Street part of Lees is now. The Bon was a separate shop then.

Barbara Phythian, born 1929

Hillsborough

Our son Colin who was born in 1970 was doing well in his job at the TSB. He was nineteen and starting to lose his pimples. He had so much to live for. On 15 April 1989 he left the house at 10.10 a.m., to go and see Liverpool play Notts Forest, in Sheffield.

My recollection is that I turned the television on and they said that the Liverpool fans had caused trouble at Hillsborough. Within ten minutes they had twenty-odd dead. I thought 'there is 10,000 people in that arena. Colin has a 10,000 to 1 chance'. But the figures went up and up. I was on my own in the house and sat there in shock. It brought back the feeling of Heysel which had happened a couple of years previously.

Finally Ian (our other son) and a friend went across to Sheffield to see if they could find him. They found him alright, but he never came back, until the Tuesday week.

We brought him home and had him in the front room. We lived virtually in a dream. We got up at seven to get washed and dressed. People would start arriving at nine o'clock and still be coming at eleven and twelve at night. They brought his clothes and money back in a bin bag. My wife and I got to the point where we were sitting on different seats afraid to talk in case we upset one another.

There were six priests at the Requiem Mass. One was on valium. Kenny Dalglish and the players were brilliant. You could not describe the love we were

The Hillsborough Memorial at Anfield.

getting from friends and family.

It is so different when you lose someone in a car accident or because of illness. You can grow out of it. But because of Hillsborough we have had to put up with the stigma that was thrown at the fans. You cannot forgive, I don't trust any policeman any more. It is a horrible thing to say. Apart from losing Colin we lost other precious things, like sincerity and telling the truth. They were looking after themselves, they tried to cop out. I lost my faith because of what happened – and in people.

Jim Wafer, born 1944

Dock Strike

When my husband, Chris, got a job on the docks, we thought it meant security for life. He worked a lot of overtime and felt he missed part of the children's childhood. But we got a car, telephone and had holidays. I started shopping at Tesco instead of Kwiksave.

Then, in 1995, the bombshell fell. He came home early and said he had been sacked. They had all been sacked. I thought it was some mistake but it went on for over two years. When I heard the real story – that five hundred dockers had been sacked after refusing to cross a picket line, I thought it was right what they were doing.

This was a different strike because the women got together. A group of dockers' wives was set up to give support. It took on a big role and became important in my life. I did not feel so alone. We supplied coffee, tea bags and butties for the picket line. It got so organised it seemed like a job. We had three years without any money coming in. We had no savings. Chris' mother used to make Sunday dinner and I would sit there and choke on it. I did not have the money to pay for it. I wonder how I bought milk, bread and nappies. The phone was cut off and Chris suffered a depression. I found work, but the stress got to me. I would run to the letter box to hide the bills; put them in my handbag and take them to work with me. It was the hardest thing in my life to tell Chris how much we owed on the mortgage. It was £600 when I told him.

The dispute ended but the dockers' wives still meet once a month. Before the strike, I thought we were safe in our own little world; now our standard of living has changed. We are on benefit. Chris is hoping for another job but our house is being repossessed and we will be living in a council house. I am resentful of the Dock Board – I have cried a river of tears.

Maria Ann Langen, born 1969

Smell

Runcorn and Widnes always had their own smell, but you were not aware of this as a child. The only time it hit me was when returning home from Anglesey, where my grandparents lived. When you came back over the bridge you realised that there was a certain smell which you had not smelled for a while. It was the butt of a lot of jokes.

David Owen, born 1966

CHAPTER 2
Getting by

Eighteen-month-old Herbert Massie, in his pram in Roxburgh Street, 1950.

Home Comforts

We lived on the top floor of an old house in Great Homer Street where I was born in 1929. The toilet was in the yard and there was no bathroom. Dad used to wrap a brick in paper and put it in the oven and then in the bed to warm it. Mum took in washing and had an iron dolly tub, and scrubbing board. I used to deliver the laundry when I was eight.

George Armstrong, born 1929

No 'Lecky'

We did not have electricity. I remember it being put in. We used gas mantles. A chap used to come round selling them from a handcart. You could also buy blocks of salt and get your knives and scissors sharpened.

John McEwan, born 1939

Flies

Everybody had fly catchers. They hung from the gas mantle and were full of flies. You were lucky if you did not get two or three in your dinner.

William Goddard, born 1894

The Pawnbroker

Everyone went to the pawnbrokers. You pawned your clothes on Monday and got them out on Friday. In 1947 when I was in the Army and stationed in North Wales, I used to come home for the weekend on Friday afternoon and pawn my boots for 3s 6d at Dalglishes on the corner of Goodison Road. Then get them out on Monday to go back.

George Armstrong, born 1929

The 'Jew Man'

The way my mother used to clothe us was the same as everyone else. You got a ticket off the Jew man. He used to be quite good. You'd get a suit and pay half a crown a week. On Monday the suit would go missing. Mother took it to the pawn shop. On Friday it came out again depending on finance. Many a time my old lady could not get it out.

Tony McGann, born 1937

The Runner

There was one lady known as the pawnshop runner: Nellie Watson. She took things to the pawn shop for others too proud to be seen going there. She always wore a man's cap with a hat pin through it.

Jack Lindo, born 1919

The Parish

We were on the parish and I remember my mother sewing uniforms of some sort, for a pittance. Once my sister found sixpence in the road and ran all the way home. My mother made a dinner from that sixpence. Sometimes my sister would take a bundle of belongings to the pawnshop and tell the pawnbroker how much my mother wanted. If he refused we would say 'Ike don't be cruel to us.' When we went back with the money we had borrowed Ike would climb the ladder and hook the parcel down from a shelf.

Lena Prince, born 1923

A Crosby Childhood

Though I was born within the sound of Bow Bells, in 1930, I moved to Crosby with my parents when I was a child. I've always thought of myself as a Scouser. We were lower middle class and lived in a semi-detached house, with a gas fire, in a cul-de-sac. My parents bought it because it was near the church. They were very thrifty and careful. I went to a convent kindergarten which was run by a French order. We called the nuns 'madame'.

Father Michael Gaine, born 1930

Water Shortage

The first house I can remember was in Tweed Street, off West Derby Road. It was three-up and three-down, a mid-Victorian terrace. If the neighbour turned her tap on, we got no water. There was strict protocol about which rooms were used. We only went in the front parlour on Sunday.

Herbert Massie, born 1949

A Home Of Our Own

When I got married I went to see Bessie Braddock (the MP for Liverpool Exchange) and she recommended me for a flat in Kirkby. But I got a bank loan for £100 to put down a deposit on a house in Huyton with Roby. Mr Noon of Herman and the Hermits lived on the same estate. It was my first dealings with a bank. The house cost £2,000 which was a lot of money. My wages were £10 a week for delivering televisions. You got 2s for putting up the aerial.

George Armstrong, born 1929

'Battling' Bessie Braddock, MP for Liverpool Exchange.

Molly Connor at the age of seventeen.

Going It Alone

We lived off Netherfield Road. My father disappeared from the face of the earth when I was twelve months old. My mother was left with four children. There was no social security. She asked for help but was told nothing could be done until he was found dead or alive. They told her to put us children in a home and herself in the workhouse. My mother said she would rather starve.

She took me on one arm and a box of kippers on the other and sold door to door. One of the things I remember about my childhood was the donkey we had. It used to pull the handcart from which my mother sold fruit and vegetables. There was one occasion when she forgot to put his nosebag on and he was half way into the house looking for his feed. In 1930, we got a shop in Netherfield Road. Mother was brilliant at buying fruit and veg in the market. She kept it in the backyard. We all had to muck in. When I was ten, I could take the donkey and deal with it. I also knew how to put my nose over a barrel of apples and tell whether there was one which was off.

Harry Mooney, born 1919

The Johnnies

Like many people who were poor in the '20s and '30s, mum was a hard worker. She would knock on doors to see if anyone wanted washing doing. She used to launder shirts for 'Johnnies.' They were on the Indian ships and today you would call them Pakistanis. 'Johnnies' was their nickname. They used to buy second-hand clothes and take them back to India and Pakistan.

George Armstrong, born 1929

Growing Up

They were good days growing up in the '30s and '40s, even though I had a pair of pumps with paper in the soles. You could leave your door open. On Saturday you could get into the pictures for a jam jar. You were ashamed if you got yourself into trouble because it brought shame on the family. There was a home for fallen women in Netherfield Road. It was run by nuns.

George Armstrong, born 1929

Playing Out

In 1943-44 we lived in a little terraced house. We'd be playing out and my mother would be sitting on the step. If something got stolen, you knew who had done it. You knew who the villain was. After the '60s came along they knocked houses down and put flats up. You did not know people. You did not know whether they were nice or a crook. There were different people from all over: Kirkby, Skem.
They did a lot of damage by moving the community. You used to be able to walk around and if you were somewhere you should not have been then someone would say: 'I'll tell your father.' We never did anything bad, like mugging. Mugging was what people did when they were buying you a drink.

Charles Jenkins, born 1937.

New Shoes

There were no big 'do's' for weddings in the '50s. Mum bought me a pair of new shoes. They sounded like boots when I walked down the aisle. You could see the price on the soles, as I knelt down. I wore my de-mob suit.

George Armstrong, born 1929

First Bathroom

I was thirty-seven before I had a bathroom, in 1964. I was all aglow. When I was growing up in Scotland Road, my mother had a flower shop with a big frontage. There was a table in the corner with oil cloth on it. She used to turn it round because of the cracks. We did not have a sink or taps. Mother used to drain the vegetables down the grid. You could wear your jersey – or gansey – for a month before washing it. The central point of our home was the fireplace. There would be an iron on the fire and you would wash your hair and sit round it while it dried.

Agnes Maddison, born 1927

Two-up and Two-down

We lived in a two-up and two-down, which was not much good for a family of thirteen. I used to sleep with my two brothers until I was fourteen. Then I slept with my mother and one

Agnes Maddison on honeymoon with husband Norman in Dublin, 1951.

baby on one side and another on the other side in a rope cot. Dad slept in the back bedroom with the boys. There was no wardrobe. We had no clothes anyway. There were two double beds in one small room. When you cleaned the room one bed had to be dismantled.

Doris Windsor, born 1917

De-bugging

Dad was a stickler for cleanliness. The legs of the beds were stuck in cans of turps or paraffin. Every Saturday dad would go round and knock the corners of the bed. Any bugs would drop into the paraffin.

Ann Roberts, born 1937

Ann Roberts, aged seven.

Cast-off Toys

Everybody was not poor. If there was only one child in the family, you could get a bike. We got cast-off toys. Someone gave me a cradle but there was no doll. I put an old sock in the cradle and rocked it. Some kids got bus tickets. We had to walk to school. Sometimes when a ticket was not being used we would be offered it. Boy, did I stand at the bus stop, preening.

Doris Windsor, born 1917

Awol

During the war, dad was in the Army, stationed in Hampshire. He heard about Liverpool getting bombed and went absent without leave. The Military Police came for him but he said he would not go back without us. So we all went; father scrubbed out an outhouse and we lived there.

Mary Jenkins, born 1940

A Comfortable Life

After injuries on the Somme, sometimes my father could not work. Mother inherited enough money to keep us afloat. Till war broke out, we had servants. A cook, nursemaid, nanny and part-time help in the garden. Blundellsands and Crosby were very comfortable places. You did not see much poverty.

William Wickham, born 1926

Toxteth

The family lived in Mulgrave Street in Toxteth when I came home from the war, in 1945. It was a beautiful street: tree-lined with red-brick houses. Granby Street was also beautiful with marvellous shops. In the 1930s the ship owners had lived there, but slowly moved away.

Jack Lindo, born 1919

Full House

There were so many of us we could not get round the table. We had dinner on the stairs. You'd have your cup on one stair and sit on another. We always got the *Echo* and dad would read it aloud as we ate. All about the Cameo murders and that sort of thing. I loved that.

Doris Windsor, born 1917

Like Sardines

We had a front parlour, an outside loo, and one main bedroom. There were ten of us. We slept top to tail in one big bed like sardines. Mum and dad slept upstairs.

Jack Lindo, born 1919

Clogs

We wore clogs in Lancashire during the week. They had leather uppers and wooden soles. On Sunday we wore proper shoes. One Sunday there was a little boy in church wearing clogs. I pointed it out and my grandmother gave me a clout for mentioning it.

John Griffin, born 1931

Keeping Clean

There were forty-seven private baths and two swimming pools in Margaret Street Baths, when I first became a baths attendant. The First Class baths cost 1s, the second class 8d. You got a brush for your back and soap and a towel for the First Class baths. If you used the cheaper ones you brought your own.

We were in Everton and not many had bathrooms. There was no stigma. People used to queue up on Sunday from seven o'clock in the morning. Wash-houses were the first places where you had a sink, back boiler and tub at the side. The dryers were called maidens. Every wash-house had a professional washer, a woman who was there from 8 a.m. until 5 p.m. She'd take the washing home, iron it and take it back to the person to whom it belonged, balancing the basket on her head.

Jack Lindo, born 1919

The Family Wash

When I was a child my mother used the wash-house. I used to go ahead and queue for a place. The clothes dried all over the house. When we moved to the tenements we hung

John Griffin and family en route to the beach at West Kirby.

the sheets on the balconies. Then my mother got her first twin tub washing machine. We used to hire one for ten bob a week. All the family would come round and take it in turns to wash.

Mary Jenkins, born 1940

Cilla's Mum

Mrs Cilla White – Cilla Black's mother – used Borough Gardens wash-house. Even when Cilla was famous she would still come to the wash-house. She was a lovely woman. Her husband Jack was lovely too. He used to stand on the corner smoking his pipe, then go for a pint or into the betting shop. When Cilla became more famous, they got a great big house in Woolton. Jack White could not stand it. He'd been taken out of his environment. He'd lived his whole life in Scotland Road where they lived over a shop.

Jack Lindo, born 1919

South Liverpool

We had a lovely home but we were not well off. Some of the stair carpets were darned. South Liverpool was a good area. Menlove Avenue, Brodie Avenue, Hornby Lane were all named after great people of Liverpool. My grandfather had a house built in Allerton Road by J.W. Jones, an established Welsh builder. We were always involved in transport. My great-uncle James had hansom cabs at the Pier Head. I still have a horse blanket with J.P. & Sons on it. My son used it at prep school. My father used to drive people like Vesta Tilley and other music hall stars around at the turn of the century.

Patrick Pearson, born 1933

Scholarship

Of the eleven children in my family they all did well. Five became school teachers and one a headmaster. This was very good considering their education. One brother got a scholarship to the grammar school but my mother took him away when he was fourteen. She said the 4s 6d he earned would help out. His headmaster was horrified and said he had Oxford potential. He went to work at Johnsons, the cleaners and used to come home like a factory boy, all blue.

Doris Windsor, born 1917

Means Test

My father died when I was sixteen. He had been gassed in the First World War where he was with the 5th Kings. His ears were badly affected, he was deaf and his eyes were sore. He had difficulty with breathing. We moved from Ruskin Street to a council house. Mother was on public assistance and was means tested. You did not get anything until you had nothing. Mr Jones was the man dealing with benefits in our area. This was the 1930s and he would come round and see what means you had. If you had hens in the backyard he would count them. Hen's eggs would feed you. Means test only allowed you the bare necessities of life.

My mother, who was proud and liked to buy furniture, had a nice dining room suite. Mr Jones came round and said she had to sell it. He lived in Muirhead Avenue and my mother would go all round the houses rather than take us anywhere near there, if we were wearing something new. We had a gramophone which she paid for weekly. Mr Jones said she had to sell that. I don't know what she got for it but we lived on that for a fortnight. Then you went back on benefit.

Vera Jeffers, born 1925

Immorality

In the old days no-one cared two hoots about getting drunk, but there was never any immorality. One woman

Doris Windsor (right) with her sister Phyllis, 1938.

came into the docks area to establish a place of ill-repute, and lasted a week. Other women drove her out; and that was as late as the 1950s. It did not mean that girls did not get pregnant – but they got married.

Father Denis McDonnell, born 1907

Affording A Dress

Crowning the May Queen was a lovely time. One year I was asked to take part in the procession but my mother could not afford the dress. My aunt May said she would buy it for me and it was lovely. Mr Jones, the Means Test man was watching and saw me. On Monday he came round and asked my mother how she had afforded the dress. It cost 9s and she had her money docked until the 9s was made up.

Vera Jeffers, born 1925

Prostitution

Liverpool did not have a big prostitution problem. There were a few married women who were hard up and disorderly houses and clubs which the police raided.

Arthur Schmuhl, born 1916

Poverty Trap

We lived in Gildard Gardens until 1968. It was a council flat slum. There were ten of us in two rooms. The only way to improve the flats was to bring them down. On Friday nights you went to the public baths. Sometimes you had the same water as the fellow in front. The conditions in which people worked were terrible. There was no health or safety. You were paid buttons. Employers would take anyone on because it was costing them next to nothing to pay them. But you had a dream – of making it out of the poverty trap.

Tony McGann, born 1937

Father Denis McDonnell at St Joseph's Church, Blundellsands, in the early 1970s.

Tony McGann (second from left, back row) with St Bridget's Catholic Young Mens' Society football team at Goodison, in 1953.

Hopscotch

Children used to keep themselves amused. They played hopscotch and skipping. Even the parents joined in. The end of the rope was tied to the lamp-post. There was not a lot of disorder. I did not know anyone with a car. Only the well off had them. Insurance people rode bikes.

John McEwan, born 1939

New Tenements

We went to live in new tenements in Sussex Gardens in Warwick Street in 1947. We had a living room, dining room with double doors, kitchen, bathroom, toilet and three bedrooms. One bedroom had a little fireplace. It was just lovely having a bath with hot water.

Mary Jenkins, born 1940

Kirkby

My parents looked after a doctor's house in Eldon Street, where I was born in 1944. We had a bath. We were fortunate. The only other house that had a bath was the priests' house. When we moved to Kirkby in 1958 we had a nice house with a bathroom, a separate toilet and four bedrooms. But my gran had a little shop in Vauxhall Road and I moved back to look after her. She had

Early advertising poster of the Overhead Railway.

two rings for cooking and big old-fashioned kettle on the side of the fire. I had to light that fire 365 days a year. There was a cold tap in the yard and you got washed there, I stayed with my gran till I got married in 1965. If you wanted to read in bed, you did so by candle light and if you did not want to take a bucket upstairs at night, you had to get up and go outside. It was not much fun if you had been drinking beer.

Jim Wafer, born 1944

Barratt Houses

Some of the old Liverpool tenements were sold to Barratts and renovated for private sales. My sister and I went to look at what had been our house. There was a lump in my throat when I saw the cupboard where we used to throw my dad's clothes. We could hardly speak. We were happy there. We moved to a pre-fab in Belle Vale, when I got married.

Mary Jenkins, born 1940

Council Flats

At one time I spent five years going to the council, trying to get a flat. This was the start of single mothers jumping the queue, and it infuriated me.

Molly Connor, born 1925

The Tribe

When they moved people to Kirkby, it did not always work. If you had what was called a 'tribe' and that tribe did not care, it was no good. We dug our gardens and tried to grow spuds. Percy Thrower would turn in his grave as to what we did. We did not have a clue. We put grass down, then played football on it, though we sometimes did wear slippers. We always kicked away from the windows because if you broke one, you paid for it.

Jim Wafer, born 1944

Nice Estate

When Norris Green was being built there was such a clamour to go and live there on a nice estate. The houses had three bedrooms and a front and back garden. My parents had their name down for several years and we got a house in Norris Green. The bathroom was downstairs and the rent was 14s a week. We moved to another house where the rent was 16s and it had an upstairs bathroom. But in Norris Green there were no shops nearby. You could not pop out to a chip shop or a pub. It was very different from living in Everton where you could walk round the corner and buy what you liked.

Arthur Schmuhl, born 1916

Viola Street

In the early '50s we got a house in Viola Street, Bootle at 16s a week. It was a lot of money and I slipped the landlord a back-hander to get it. We never bought anything on tick. We got a radiogramme for £87. It played eight records and was a

The corner of Lord Street and Whitechapel, 1908.

seven-day wonder. I used to polish it and sit and stare at it. I loved Andy Williams and the Beatles. Eventually I got a vacuum cleaner. Before that you brushed a lot. We also had a water geyser in Viola Street.

Agnes Maddison, born 1927

Cousin Grace

My cousin Grace got married and went to America. She came back in 1960 with a baby in paper nappies. We thought it was disgusting. She used to use Gordon Moore toothpaste which was probably American. Her gums were always bright red and her teeth very white.

Ann Roberts, born 1937

Chauffeur Driven

My mother caught Russian flu in 1916 and the doctor said she had to live out of Liverpool to protect her chest. So we moved to Hoylake. We lived there for forty-eight years. We were well-off. Father died in 1959 and I used to look at old balance sheets. We had hundreds of pounds. In 1923 we had two servants. One called Martha and Mary Lynch, who was a good little cook. They slept upstairs. The family slept on the first floor. There were three living rooms which were quite comfortable and long corridors with lino. No central heating. There was no Mersey Tunnel in those days. The chauffeur drove father to Hamilton Square where he got the train to James Street and then walked down Lord Street. Liverpool merchants lived the good life without thought for others.

David Solomon, born 1916

Automatic

When we got a pre-fab we also got our first automatic washing machine. We were too scared to leave it to work on its own, We were not convinced we could put the clothes and washing powder in and forget about it.

Mary Jenkins, born 1940

First Car

In 1942 we got our first car and paid cash. It was a little mini and it was the cream on the flipping cake. I used to look out of the bedroom window and stare at it, hypnotised. The impossible had come true.

Agnes Maddison, born 1927

Big Influence

The washing machine has been one of the biggest influences on women's lives. When it arrived, the fridge also changed things. It meant you did not have to shop each day.

Mary Jenkins, born 1940

Redundant

In 1990, my husband Robert was made redundant after over thirty years with the same company. We paid off the mortgage with his redundancy money and had £12,000 left. A financial adviser told us how to invest it. It seemed a fortune to us but, of course, Robert was not working. It made me so proud when he took a job cleaning the toilets at the University for £48 a week.

Ann Roberts aged seven, with neighbours in Prescot Street, now the site of the Royal Hospital.

It meant he could keep his car. Then he got a job as a porter.

Ann Roberts, born 1937

Chinese Laundry

You saw few black faces or Oriental children in Park Road where I grew up. My dad was Chinese and my mother half Chinese. I was born in the laundry they ran. My father had this dream of making enough money to take us all back to Hong Kong, but we did not speak or write Chinese so we would have had a struggle. He spoke pidgin English and his whole idea was that we should all get degrees. He sent money home to Hong Kong regularly and would borrow to do so rather than lose face. In Hong Kong he was considered a success because in England he had his own business.

Susan Grainger, born 1948

Credit Union

Somewhere along the line, someone introduced us to the Credit Union and all the mums in Speke saved up. It was brilliant and led to our first holiday. You save for twelve weeks by which time you must have paid in £67. After that you are allowed a loan of £200. While you are paying that back, you pay a pound or two into shares. So as your loan is coming down your shares are going up. Once you have paid that off, your next loan is £500. You have to

Mobile advertising in Crosshall Street, 1953.

have £250 in to get that. To borrow £1,000 you have to have £500.

Amanda Brown, born 1964

The 'Cattie'

Most of my money went into paying off the catalogue and home shopping, I was up to my eyes in it. I also got in with Provident. They lend you money but once you pay it back they ask you if you want another loan. You say yes, because you need it. It's a case of robbing one to pay another.

Yvonne Puran, born 1964

Loan Sharks

Without the Credit Union we'd be lost. Loan sharks are a problem though I have never been involved with them myself. But there are people who are desperate enough to give them their benefit books.

Yvonne Puran, born 1964

Teaching

The toughest time of my life was teaching at St Kevin's comprehensive in Kirkby.

When I went there in 1962 there were 2,000 boys and 2,000 boys for assembly is a frightening sight. The school had fourteen streams and the lower forms were virtually ineducable. They did something called rural studies which meant they went out in the morning and dug a hole in a field. In the afternoon they filled it in. It was as bad as that. Occasionally a teacher would send them to the bookies. They might not know how to do sums, but they knew how to deal with bookies.

Father Michael Gaine, born 1930

Paddling

We all helped in our Chinese laundry. The clothes were put into a soaking vat and we used to dance – or paddle – on them.

Susan Grainger, born 1948

Sausages On Sticks

Our first house was a three-bedroomed sunshine semi in Bowring Park, for £2,400. People had lots of parties in their homes, with meat pies and sausages on sticks. We never discovered any wife swapping. It was all quite moral. Before we were married we went on holiday to Italy, by train. It cost £24 and was a fantastic experience. The weather, the food was different from anything I had known.

Ann Williams, born 1939

First Bath

Until I went to teacher training college at nineteen in 1969, I had never had a bath. At our house in Park Road we washed in the sink. When I married and moved to Childwall where

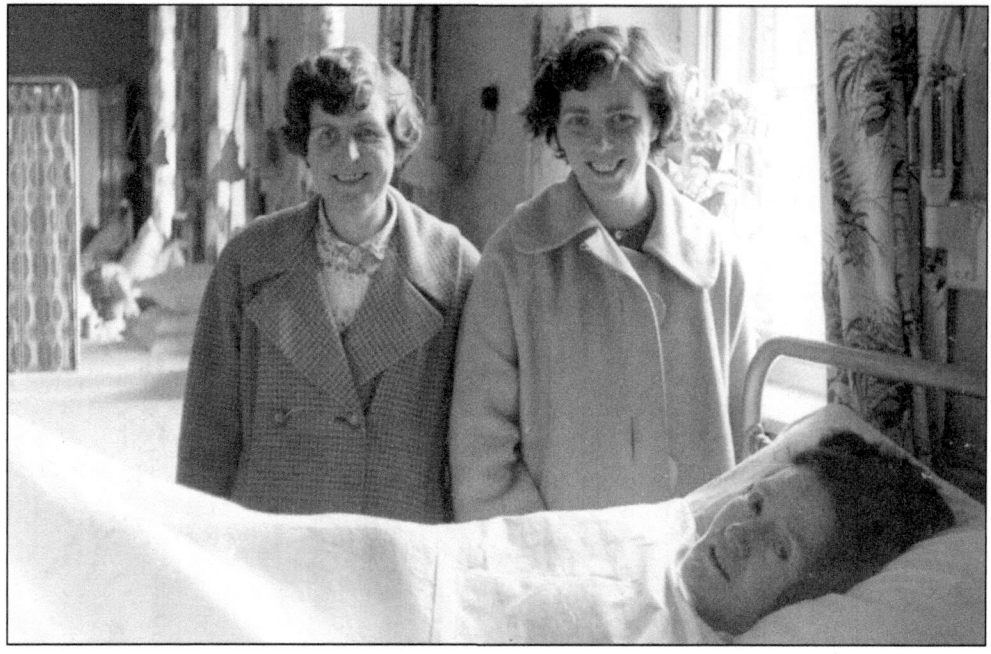

Hospital visiting in Durham, 1959. Lena Prince (left) was training to be a lay reader.

we bought a semi with three bedrooms and a bathroom, I was aware I was going up in life. In 1988 we went to live in Fulwood Park which runs down to the Mersey and is made up of large sandstone houses, built at the turn of the century, owned by shipping people. Ours is a modern house. We bought it because I wanted a bigger kitchen.

Susan Grainger, born 1948

Housewife

We were married six years before we had children and moved to Southport. In my day you did not go back to work, because you wanted to stay with them. This was when I discovered the value of the Housewives' Register – a network of women who met in each other's homes. It was a very significant part of my married life. Talk of nappies and babies was banned. Women were thinking of doing something with their lives. By this time I had middle class aspirations.

By 1972 I was into the pro-abortion movement. I felt very passionately about women having the right to choose. The British Pregnancy Association were looking for a Counsellor and when I was thirty-nine, I became mature student, and did a sociology course. For the first time I had domestic help, but I tended to clean the house before the cleaner came! I felt very guilty that someone else was doing my housework but I wanted to do well at the university and did not want to cope with everything. My husband did most of the shopping, cooking and child care.

Ann Williams, born 1939

CHAPTER 3
Work and play

The traditional May Day celebrations.

Cammell Laird

It was 1934 and the middle of the Depression, when I got my first job. I was fourteen. At school, if you got eighty points in an exam you went to Technical College, if you got ninety you went to college, I got seventy-six. I began working for Mr Myers in Great Homer Street as a butcher's messenger. I had a bike with a small wheel in front and a basket at the front where the meat was carried. I got 5s a week but in those days they used to sack you at sixteen because they had to give you a rise.

My sister got me a job at Owen Owen as a porter. My floor was the basement. All the china was on the floor. If you broke it, there was your wage gone. Eventually I got a trade at Cammell Laird, first as a plumber's labourer, then a driller at 15s a week. It was a tough job being under a ship on the stocks. You were issued with tools but if you lost them you had to replace them. If you were off work ill, you had to do time to make it up. Everyone was proud of working at Cammell Laird Shipyard. Every time a ship went down the stocks, a part of you went with it. You took a pride in building a ship.

Harry Mooney, born 1919

Overtime

You were on a treadmill working at the Meccano factory. On Tuesday, Wednesday and Thursday you had to work until eight o'clock at night. It was compulsory. I needed the money to pay for the flat I had in Gresham Street, which cost 37s a week. I also had to pay for my keep and I was saving up to get married.

Ann Roberts, born 1937

Dolls

My first job was in Duke Street at a place where they made dolls. I had to carry the dolls heads to be dipped in wax. I hated it.

Molly Connor, born 1925

Molly Connor (thirty) relaxes in Rhyl, 1957.

Liverpool tenements in the 1930s.

An experiment in keeping in touch with what was going on outside the ground at Goodison Park, 1953. Sergeant Arthur Schmuhl is on the right.

Bananas

Around 1933 when I was fourteen I left school and became a grocery errand boy on a bike. At fifteen I went to Yeowards, fruit merchants, in Park Lane and stuck labels on bananas. After that I went to the Co-op and sold ice cream from one of those tricycles. You got 24s a week and commission on what you sold. During the war, I was with Wingate's Chindits, as they called them. We operated behind the Japanese lines. I came out with a long beard and hair down my neck, You could not shave.

Jack Lindo, born 1919

Name Change

There were 750 interviewed, and only 36 accepted, when I joined the police in 1937. The Chief Constable, who had the last say, said I had done well and was going to be accepted, provided I changed my name. I told him that as I was only twenty I would have to ask my dad. When I did, he said, as he himself had been good enough to fight for the 5th Kings with the name Schmuhl, he would not give his permission. I never did change my name.

Arthur Schmuhl, born 1916

Thetis

It was a terrible thing when the *Thetis* was sunk in June, 1939. I'd worked on it and you knew people who went down with her. I was a driller when she was on the stocks, then she moved to the fitting out basin for trials in Liverpool Bay. All sailors on deck were in white ducks, it being June. As the Thetis went out into the river, we all cheered it on its way.

The following morning, going to work they were selling newspapers with the headlines 'Submarine Down in Liverpool Bay.' You just could not believe that it was the *Thetis*, but it was. I have heard so many stories but the truth, as far as I know, is that they eventually tried to raise the stern end of the *Thetis* and got four tugs to hold it. The idea was to cut the tail end and get the men out. Cammell Laird thought that was the best thing. But the Navy had taken the vessel over and the Navy were in charge. My mate, Jim Lawrenson, was the driller and he went out to cut the hole in it. There was a boat belonging to the Mersey Docks and Harbour Board, called the *Salver*, with all the drilling gear, to either cut it or burn it out with an oxyocetaline burner, but the Admiralty did not want to damage the vessel.

Cammell Laird and the Admiralty had meeting after meeting and in the end, they said no holes had to be cut. I can remember the pictures, in the paper, of the vessel jutting out of the water, but when the tide came in, the tugs could not hold her any more, and they had to let her go. There were four men who escaped. One man was the foreman fitter and his hair went white. I never saw anything like it. It was a terrible thing to happen, because you knew a lot who went down with her, including tradesmen. Whenever a ship went on its trials, they always took tradesmen with them, in case anything went wrong, then they would be there to repair the damage or whatever. So a lot of tradesmen went. I could have gone, but I turned the offer down, not because I thought it was a case of taking a chance, but because I thought it was beyond me. I was just turned eighteen. Jim Lawrenson, with whom I was working, also refused to go, but when the tragedy happened, he was called out to do the job. He was a good driller and knew exactly what was wanted.

Eventually when the war had started, the following November, they had an old trans-ship in Cammell Laird and they put timber beams across the deck and went out to try and raise the *Thetis*. The timber beams broke, so they made steel box girders and slung them under the submarine. As the tide came in, they lifted it up. They spent a number of days doing this till they got it on shore. Then they opened it up – the men were all buried in Anglesey and the *Thetis* was brought into Camell Laird, refurbished, and brought up to date. It was like going to a ghost ship, because you could not help but think of all the men who had died in her. But, like everything else, you had to get on with the job. The war was on.

Harry Mooney, born 1919

Ill Feeling

There was a bit of ill feeling between me and my father when I joined the police force in 1937. He had spent at least thirty years as a qualified French polisher and was on the maximum pay of £2 10s a week. In the police I got £3 10s as a lad of twenty. I am amazed at what the police earn now. Then it was not the seriousness of the offence but the number. If you could pinch a dozen fellows during the week for setting off fireworks or playing football or cards in the street, it was much better than locking a person up for shop lifting, which was a serious crime.

Arthur Schmuhl, born 1916

Accidents

At Laird's, it was part of the job for things to fall on you. There were so many accidents that Cammell Laird had its own ambulance. They said it did not need a driver, it could find its own way to Birkenhead General Hospital. At Cammell Laird you were allowed three minutes to go to the toilet. It was hard luck if you had diarrhoea. You got your pay docked.

Harry Mooney, born 1919

Pay Packet

It was a joy to be working. When I was at Pecks making overalls in the '40s I only got 5s a week. I gave my wage packet to my mother unopened and she gave me sixpence.

Agnes Maddison, born 1927

Jobs

In Liverpool, as elsewhere, Jewish people followed three main trades: furniture making, money lending and tailoring. Mother wanted me to be a stockbroker but I was determined, like my father, to go into the furniture trade because I knew it was a good living. Mother went to school with one of the Sieff family so I got an opening with Marks and Spencer in Liverpool. But I went into the family business after the war. I earned £15 a week.

David Solomon, born 1916

War Work

In 1939 I was conscripted and went into an aircraft factory at Speke. We were taught how to put rivets on fusilages of Halifax bombers. We wore bib and braces overalls and climbed ladders; did shift work. We earned £42 a week which was a lot of money in those days.

Lena Prince, born 1923

Judge William Wickham seen as a baby with his mother, Mary.

University Grant

In 1945, the government offered to pay full fees and a maintenance grant for any ex-serviceman or woman, at any university they could get into. I had gone into the Army when I left Sedburgh School in 1944. It seemed a better idea to go to Oxford rather than Liverpool University which had been the original idea, so I went to Brasenose College for an interview. I don't think I learned any more there than I would have done at Liverpool but it was more fun and more exciting.

It was around the age of sixteen that I had decided that it seemed a good idea to go to the Bar. I felt it was something I would be good at. I suppose I was attracted to the idea of standing up in court – not really a good reason for going to the Bar. I did not want to spend all day sitting in an office. It was my ambition to become a judge, because I thought it would be marvellous – which it was. At the end of twenty-two years, I had a reputation as a fierce sentencer. I am sorry about that. I would rather have liked to have a reputation as an efficient judge.

William Wickham, born 1926

John Lennon

One of my great pleasures was to give John Lennon a smack over the mouth. It was around 1963-64 and the Orange Lodge had a service on St

Rose Heilbron, Liverpool's most famous woman lawyer.

George's plateau. I was a police inspector by then. There was a fellow dancing up and down on the glass canopy over the Empire Theatre opposite, waving to the crowd. I went over and told him he was a stupid so-and-so and should come in but he told me to f*** off.

I completely lost my rag, stepped out onto the glass canopy, and smacked him, across the mouth. It was John Lennon; the Beatles were giving an interview. I've heard all sorts of talk about Lennon, but he was a foul mouthed gutter-snipe in my opinion.

Arthur Schmuhl, born 1916

Opium

In 1961 there were fourteen men on the police Vice Squad, two men dealing with drugs. Today's drug squad consists of fifty men. The only drug around then was opium. There were four Chinese places in Nelson Street, where the older Chinese used to smoke. They used beautiful Chinese pipes and seemed to go into a dream.

They never encouraged young people, but now and again we had to raid them. I hated doing this because I did not think they were doing anything wrong. But it was against the law. I was never happy with the idea of women police officers. When you got things like strikes you were more concerned with their safety than doing your job. At first we had two in the Vice Squad. They were policewomen but basically did the typing.

Arthur Schmuhl, born 1916

The Portia Factor

In the '50s and '60s Rose Heilbron who was, in some sense, Liverpool's favourite daughter, was the only woman silk in practice. She was not accepted by the Northern Circuit for a long time. Rose was defeated for the leadership of the Northern Circuit by a much junior male silk though she did eventually become leader. She was not allowed to 'mess' (dine) with the men silks. But by the 1970s there were a lot more women coming to the Bar.

William Wickham, born 1926

First Job

The first day after I left school my old lady took me to the old barrel yard. I was fifteen and I worked on two big boilers and there was a caustic tank which reconditioned oil drums. I've never been out of work in my life and stayed in one job as a fork lift driver for twenty-two years.

Tony McGann, born 1937

Littlewoods

You had to pass a general knowledge test to get a job at Littlewoods. I started there when I was sixteen and earned £5 a week. When I left Littlewoods I had married and was four months pregnant. I thought babies came out of your belly button.

Agnes Maddison, born 1927

Nineteen-year-old Stan Soudet (left) seen with friends in Durban in 1942, while he was in the Royal Navy.

Wages

If you worked for Littlewoods you were well paid. When I started there I got more wages than my dad got on the docks. Littlewoods was good to work for. You got breaks: cups of tea, cheap meals. I loved it.

Mary Jenkins, born 1940

No Work

From 1929, my dad did not work for seven years because of the Depression. He went out every evening for a drink and smoked Capstan Extra Strength. He loved my mother and used to sing to her. We were poor but there was this feeling of unity. We felt secure.

Agnes Maddison, born 1927

Clippie

My mum became a clippie on the trams during the war. I used to walk to Spelling Lane and she would come on the No. 3 tram. She gave me sixpence at the terminus. She also worked in a munitions factory near Jacobs. Dad was unemployed but eventually got a job in a snooker hall in Foley Street by Lawrence Road where the old tram sheds were. There were two tables.

George Armstrong, born 1929

Fords

After the Overhead closed I went to work as a conductor on the No. 1 bus on the Dock Road. I knew all the dockers again and was there for five years. Then in the early '60s I went to Fords and stayed for seventeen and half years. People thought that if you worked at Fords you were making hundreds. I went home with about £27 a week, which was better than average. I was there during the ten week strike and it was bad. Everyone was in the union, the Transport and General. The picket line was hand picked. When I went to the UAB in Penny Lane, to ask for some money, they said I was not entitled to anything but you could have money for your wife and children.

Stan Soudet, born 1922

Going To Sea

Everyone wanted to go to sea but you really had to be fifteen and a half. I ran away at fourteen. I took my mum's gas mask and left a note saying I had gone to sea. I was the pantry boy, peeling spuds on a cargo boat going round the coast.

George Armstrong, born 1929

Scholarship

Though almost every man where I was born worked in the colliery, my father said I was not going down the mine. I got a scholarship to the grammar school and wanted to be a teacher. I was all set to go the university but felt honour bound not to, due to family finance. In 1949 I passed the exam into the Civil Service and ended up as Regional Controller of the North West Region of the Department of Health and Security.

John Griffin, born 1931

Abattoir

The slaughterhouse at the abattoir was full of steam and dead animals and blood. Like anything else, you got used to it. It never put me off meat but I will not eat veal, if I can help it. The little calves were killed by hooking them up to a ring, upside down, slitting their throats and letting them bleed to death. It made the meat white. I could not cope with that. The men who worked there were a tough breed. If you were a new boy like me, earning £5 a week, they'd hang a pair of ears or something else on your bike. As a joke they sent me to a butchers suppliers in Prescot Road, to ask for a bag of chickens' lips.

Michael Penn, born 1945

Barry Casey, Ann Roberts' nephew, with his father James at Smithdown Lane, c. 1956.

Tom Eccleston at his desk, 1968.

Ogdens

Once you started working at Ogdens, the tobacco company, you soon got to know how to weigh tobacco in the hand. You'd take a handful and know that it was around a couple of ounces. You'd throw it in a bucket and eventually it would be packed as pipe tobacco. We wore turbans and underneath we put curlers in our hair, covered by a hair net. You were not supposed to in case they fell into the tobacco.

Discipline was very strict. There was a lady called Nancy Tighter who was very tall and straight with her hair plaited in ear-phones. One day she came storming down the room with a packet of tobacco. Someone's hairnet had ended up in a packet and been found by the poor man who opened it.

Then, though we worked with tobacco we were not aware that smoking could be dangerous. Father used to say it stunted your growth. If you were told that you did not listen. A portable bus came round and everyone had to be X-rayed. A lot of people had to leave with TB and go into the sanatorium. We used to wonder if smoking caused TB.

Barbara Harrison, born 1937

Cinderella

Thirty years ago, when you started working with the DSS, the first thing you were issued with was a pen, a towel and a piece of soap. Plus galoshes and a sweater to wear if you were out visiting. We were the Cinderella Department and the clientele were very different.

People were not unemployed for long. If you were it was because you were bone idle. Very few owned their own houses. The fiddlers have always been with us. When I began it was small stuff. There were a lot of window cleaners with wives earning a few bob at the pub. Now we have criminals who target security.

Tom Eccleston, born 1948

Stigma

We were taught to try and get rid of the stigma of public assistance when I first became a Social Security official, but it was there. In those days every client was visited at home. This was before Giro cheques came in and people were paid in cash.

John Griffin, born 1931

Widnes

Widnes, where I was born, is only twelve miles from Liverpool, yet people speak with a different accent and play a different sport. It is seen as quaintly Lancastrian to want to play rugby league, especially as down the road in Liverpool there are two of the most successful football teams in the world. But over the years some things have changed in Widnes. Thirty years ago it was a northern town, trying to find and identify itself having been very much at the forefront of the chemical industry, world-wide. As far as global economic issues were concerned, chemicals became less and less important and it was easier and easier to make them more cheaply. So you had predominantly a workforce who had been educated to expect to work in the chemical industry and also, to a certain extent, to have a job there for life. They had to change their pattern of work which had been replicated around the north of England in particular.

I was at school with boys whose parents were working in industry but fewer from my generation went on themselves to work in these traditional jobs. Though perhaps their fathers were second or third generation even working for the same company.

David Owen, born 1966

Freezing

In winter St George's Hall, where the courts were, was freezing. I dare say it was intimidating for ordinary persons going into court. Then in 1984 the new Palace of Justice, in Derby Square, was opened with twenty-eight courts.

William Wickham, born 1926

Education

The comprehensive school I went to had between 1,200 and 1,600 pupils but the size was not a problem. There was no bullying and there were children from all walks of life. There were not the pressures to go on to further education that there are today. Before I went to Liverpool University to read law, I spent two years at a sixth form college. It was the most liberal and important part of my academic career. You were treated like an adult.

In the 1980s student life was a little more carefree than it is now. When I was at university, I never had to worry about finances and I think that was the same for the majority of my contemporaries, irrespective of whether they needed assistance from the government or their parents. But the cost of being a student was less than it is now and there was more opportunity to find work through the summer or even

The sixth form history class at Sedburgh School 1943. William Wickham is on the front row, first on the left.

during term time, which does not exist now. You could become a builder's mate, pick beans, many things.

David Owen, born 1966

No Jobs

At one time everyone seemed to be on a Youth Opportunity Scheme but there were no jobs. For twelve months you got reduced pay of about £30 a week.

Yvonne Puran, born 1964

Left School

The Youth Opportunity Scheme had just come in when I left school at sixteen in 1980. I went on one but, after that, never bothered. My first baby was born when I was nineteen and I had four kids, all by the same dad. Now, I am a Credit Union Loans Officer and interview people who need to raise money. There was one girl whose husband had died. She needed money for food, for clothes and for a headstone for her husband's grave.

Amanda Brown, born 1964

Liverpool Stock Exchange

When I graduated from Liverpool University in 1987. I decided that law was not for me, so I sat down and discussed it with my father. I had always been interested in economics and the business world. I started on that career in October of that year and, as any stock market historian will tell you, there was the largest stock market crash two weeks later. An interesting time to start your career.

One of the great financial myths is that Liverpool is not an obvious place for a stock market. But if you look at the history of the city, you will see that it was built on trading. Buying and selling shares is another form of trading. Until 1986, the Liverpool Stock Market had a floor where people shouted at each other and bought and sold shares. Then it changed to an electronic dealing system where everybody dealt off a computer screen. With the aid of my computer, I can get to know what has happened in the world as quickly as anyone else, no matter where it is.

David Owen, born 1966

Marbles

As children at the turn of the century, we used to play 'stonies' – marbles. It must have been around 1908 when the cinemas came to Widnes. I was fourteen. The best seats cost two pence – up in the gallery. If you got on the front row there were no blooming big hats in front of you. They were silent films but, looking back, it did not seem long before they were talking.

William Goddard, born 1894

How to plan for the future.

Fashion

At the beginning of the century my mother wore long skirts which touched the pavement. To combat the dust they had brush braid at the hem. There was also a loop at the back to hold the skirt up. She made me dresses in a fabric called Holland and they were embroidered with cross stitch.

Women wore corsets and bras, which were actually just pieces of lace tied at the front. They did not have cups. Mother's hats were wonderful, great wide things. One was of wine-coloured velvet trimmed with a diamanté brooch and a couple of roses. Hair then was always long, often down to your waist. There were no hair dryers, so it took forever to dry.

Madge Parry, born 1899

Growing Up

Over in Wirral we roller skated on the promenade, played hockey and went to the baths when we were growing up in the '30s. It was a good time for those with money but we were not aware of it. We did not realise that children went to school in bare feet. You could get a student ticket to travel to Juan le Pins for £12.50. If you went to a brothel it was not a place with naked women wanting to take you to bed. There'd be a long bar and a girl would come and sit next to you and say 'Buy me a grog.' Those who wanted to made arrangements and disappeared upstairs for a bit. I'd say that in ninety per cent of cases it was domestic servants who took your virginity. That's what happened to me. I was fifteen.

David Solomon, born 1916

The 'Graffie'

We used to go dancing at the Grafton and the Richmond School of Dancing in Breck Road. The teacher, Mr Campbell, took the part of the lady and taught me how to guide her around the dance floor, by placing a hand in the middle of her back and guiding her to left and right. You don't see that today. You wore your best suit and tie to go dancing. I looked for second-hand dancing shoes in Paddy's Market and got them for about sixpence. They were patent leather and I polished them like mad.

Harry Mooney, born 1919

Jewish Boys

Jewish boys rarely drank to oblivion because you knew you always had to have one eye over your shoulder. You knew you could not protect yourself if you had too much to drink. We drank at Yates Wine Lodge. If you bought Yates tarragona red wine, put an egg-cupful of methylated spirits in it, and shook it up, it gave you a good lift. It did not do you any harm.

David Solomon, born 1916

Bold Street in its heyday, c. 1950.

Mascara

Mascara was the first cosmetic I started wearing. I could not wear anything else because of my dad. My mum used it. She would never go anywhere without her eyelashes being done. She'd spit on the brush then rub it into the mascara.

Maria Ann Langan, born 1969

The Cavern

As well as Reeces, the Locarno and the Grafton we went to the Cavern at lunchtime and to listen to jazz at the Temple on Sunday. Around the age of seventeen, you felt that you had become an adult. It was the '60s and I was into fashion and used to make my own clothes. I would knock something up on Friday to wear on

Saturday. Skirts then, were bouffant, with lots of petticoats. I preferred it when the sack came in. I never had any bosom so I used to shove any old thing down my bra. We wore stockings and suspenders. Make-up was panstick with big eyes and white lips. There was no sex education. When I started my periods I did not know what was happening.

Anne Williams, born 1939

Short Trousers

I went to school in short trousers and a gabardine mac with mittens with strings through the arms. The 1960s was the break point where you stopped wearing a scaled down version of what your dad wore. Girls wore scaled down versions of their mums' clothes. The '60s fashion was for the young. Austin Reed was the young mans' tailor. I was pretty good with a needle and cotton and used to alter my clothes. I made some of my trousers narrower than when they were bought, to my mum's disgust. The Beatles introduced Cuban heeled boots.

Tom Eccleston, born 1948

Winkle Pickers

Winkle picker shoes are something I will never forget. They were so long. I remember seeing one boy come down the stairs of a bus walking sideways, like a crab, because that was the only way his feet would fit on the stairs. The mohair teddy boy suits, with their velvet collars, always seemed like period costume to me.

Barbara Phythian, born 1929

Love And Marriage

It was love at first sight when I met my wife at Grove Street Jewish Club. Her engagement ring was a two stone diamond. We were married in 1941 when I was on leave from the Army. I told her that if we lost the war to get a stone taken out and use it for passage to New York. New York was full of pawnbrokers and she could use the other stone to raise money. I also told her to go to the Walford Astoria every month and I would use it as a *poste restante*. But it did not come to that.

David Solomon, born 1916

Buses

Before the war, when we went into town, all we did was window shop. After the war, stores like Lees and Blacklers built up. Trams gave way to buses.

Jack Lindo, born 1919

Clothing Coupons

During the war when there was clothes rationing, you needed one and a half coupons for a pair of stockings. Nylons were not out then. The nicest stockings were made of pure silk and fully fashioned. Ordinary stockings were of rayon. Fully fashioned stockings had seams up the back and were lovely. I liked them because they gave your leg more shape.

Vera Jeffers, born 1925

Make-up

During the war and after, you made do and mend as far as make-up was concerned. For my eyebrows I'd strike a match, put it out, then draw them in with the burnt end. For our legs, we used leg tan and drew a black line up the back. Earrings were made out of buttons.

When I was courting I had to be in at 11 p.m. I bought my wedding dress from another girl for £10. The veil was stiff. There were two bridesmaids, one in pink, one in blue. On my wedding day, I took my towel and soap and went to the public baths, to 'wash all over' and put curlers in my hair. The water in the baths used to come out scalding.

Agnes Maddison, born 1927

Our Shop

Woolworths was our shop. I used to buy bottles of perfume for sixpence, on behalf of my brother, to

Vera Jeffers (front row, first on left) as train bearer to the May Queen at St Theresa's church, Norris Green, 1939.

Vera Jeffers' auntie May returns via helicopter with other fashion buyers from a trip to London Hosiery Week, 1964. Auntie May wears a beaded hat.

give to his girlfriend.

Lena Prince, born 1923

The '50s and '60s

Life as a single man in the '50s and '60s included a lot of playing records. There was Frankie Laine, Eddy Fisher, Guy Mitchell. I've still got the old records. I could not dance – I was like a horse trampling in manure. Boxing was popular. It was a good way of occupying yourself.

Tony McGann, born 1937

Three Course Lunch

There was a large Co-op, at Unity House where the university is now, you could get a three course lunch for 1s 9d. After that you went to the Trocadero in Fraser Street to see a film; or the Paramount or Majestic. You always went out on Saturday afternoon and Saturday night.

Lena Prince, born 1923

The Flicks

Things in the cinema industry changed drastically when television came along. From my schooldays I always had a fixation to go into the film business due, no doubt, to my father's involvement. He was the assistant manager at the Olympia in West Derby at the time of the first talkie, *The Jazz Singer*. The cinema business always seemed to be glamorous. My feeling was that people went because it took them out of their mundane lives. They saw things they had no chance of experiencing, which was why they flocked to the cinema in their thousands. There was none of the sex and violence you see today. Films like *Saturday Night* and *Sunday Morning* were a turning point. Liverpool had a flourishing cinema business but as television became more popular, people turned their backs on the cinema. Like everywhere else Liverpool's cinemas turned into bingo halls.

Gerry Lipson, born 1929

Colour Telly

I remember the day we got colour telly. Mum picked me up from school and said 'There's a surprise when you get home.' My sister spoiled it by shouting from the other side of the road 'We've got colour telly.' The first video I watched was *E.T.*

In the pub we'd make one glass of lager last all night. I began going to clubs when I was seventeen. They were huge and dark with flashing lights. Now and then I'd buy a bottle of malibu and go to my friend Lorraine's house. I'd get a bath and made up there. Sometimes we'd take the bottle with us and knock it back in the toilets at the dance hall. We'd dance facing each other with our handbags on the floor.

Maria Ann Langan, born 1969

In The Park

In the late 1940s life was a big adventure. We used to go to Calderstones Park and come home exhausted.

John McEwan, born 1939

Dancing

People went dancing a lot in the '50s. You would see well over a thousand dancing at the Grafton.

George Armstrong, born 1929

Elvis

At the start of the '50s, Elvis Presley came on the scene. Fashion became important. You could get a suit made for £10 and a Crombie coat for the same price. We wore winkle pickers and boot-lace ties. There was a tailor called Beno Dorn who won an award for tailor of the year. It was a time of crew cuts and there was a hairdresser called Max, the mad Russian.

John McEwan, born 1939

Rock 'n Roll

When we used to go dancing, it was the time of rock and roll, and

Little Richard. We all had our eye on someone. We went somewhere because he was there. It was very innocent. You never asked a boy to dance. You thought that if he put his tongue in your mouth you could have a baby.

Mary Jenkins, born 1940

Best Bands

In its heyday, the Grafton had the best bands. Joe Loss, Ted Heath, Jack Parnell as well as people like Ray Ellington appeared there. Those were the days.

Charles Jenkins, born 1937

Diana Dawson aged eight, in Vale Park, New Brighton, 1947.

Bidston Hill

Going to Bidston Hill was a big adventure. So was going into town.

Diana Dawson, born 1939

Cuckoo Clock

Once upon a time Woolton was considered to be the country. We used to go and see the cuckoo clock in Woolton Woods. It was wonderful: a large clock face done with flowers. Children were safe on the streets. We played on the embankment at Sefton Park Station and went into the Mystery at Greenbank Park. There were benches where our mothers sat.

Gerry Lipson, born 1929

School Caps

If you were seen going to school without a cap, your name was put on the board as a 'Capless Cretin'. Mine frequently appeared there. You did not wear long pants until you were about thirteen or fourteen, which meant you had chapped legs in winter and grazed knees.

Michael Penn, born 1945

The Match

Football was always important in Liverpool. When we got into the car after our wedding, my new husband

Gerry Lipson while on National Service with the RAF at Warrington Station, 1947.

asked the driver 'Who won the match?' Not very romantic.

Ann Roberts, born 1937

Doorman

In 1955, I got a job as a doorman at the Locarno. The wages were 7s 6d a night. I was told that if I got myself a bow tie I could start that night. I never looked back. The Beatles played at both the Grafton at the Locarno. Brian Epstein, their manager, was there and I had a coffee with him.

George Armstrong, born 1929

Rolling Stones

There was not much for teenagers in St Helens. I remember watching the Rolling Stones live at Wigan Empire in the '60s.

There was nothing like a trip to the pictures for a kiss and cuddle.

Tom Eccleston, born 1948

Gramophone

Being fond of dancing I loved our gramophone. It stood on four legs and you wound it up. I used to put *Tip Toe Through the Tulips* and *Springtime in the Rockies* on and dance around.

Vera Jeffers, born 1925

The Royal Iris

Sailing out to the bar on the Royal Iris and back again was fun. Though it was more like a cargo ship than a cruise ship.

Anne Williams, born 1939

Youth Club

The Youth Club was the centre of our lives. I vividly remember starching my underskirt for the Saturday night dance in the Church Hall. You soaked it in sugar and dried it in the airing cupboard until it was stiff. It had to be done when mum was out and you could pinch the sugar. The first make-up I used was Ponds and the first lipstick was called 'Natural.' It looked orange but it had no colour. You buffed your nails to make them shine. At school I was the last person in my year to wear a bra.

Josephine Humphries, born 1942

New Brighton

In summer we went to New Brighton baths. It was an open-air pool with a lounge area and was very much a meeting place for young people. I had a leopard-skin bikini and I can remember dancing around in it and making a complete fool of myself. Swimming was an also-ran. You were there to be seen. I had high heels and a beehive hair-do to make myself look taller. We used a mixture of olive oil and lemon, to make ourselves fry. We

Lena Prince receives an award from Robert Runcie for the Radio Merseyside programme about her life, *Lena's Story*, 1995.

did not know the consequences.

Anne Williams, born 1939

Liverpool and Everton

Our family were mixed in supporting both Liverpool and Everton football teams but mainly Liverpool. The ornaments on the mantelpiece would be draped in black if Liverpool had been knocked out at a Wembley final. When I went to my first match at Anfield I could not get over how close I was to the players. Before I got a season ticket I used to go in the Anfield Road stand on my own. When Liverpool scored everyone surged forward and I once lost my specs and a button off my jacket. The singing was louder then and you did not have the bad language. Hillsborough has helped. There is not the mad scramble coming out and more courtesy towards women.

Lena Prince, born 1923

Autographs

Attitudes to football have changed. When Billy Liddell was my idol you did not get involved in autograph hunting. You went to the match; then you went home. It is different now. Then it was the sport you went to see, now there is so much hype and it is so expensive you cannot afford to go unless you have £30 or £40 to spare. Going to the match used to be a day out. You'd get yourself washed and dressed and put on a clean shirt. You did not go out scruffy. But we played a lot of sport ourselves. I did not bother with girls till I was eighteen. I was too busy playing football. There was badminton on Monday and Wednesday, table tennis on Tuesday and Thursday and snooker till eight o'clock on Friday, then you went for a couple of drinks.

Jim Wafer, born 1944

Everton

My mother was always a devoted Evertonian, so I used to be taken to the match when I was two or three. I loved it. We were in the stands. I sat on her knee. My grandparents lived in Walton and we went there and walked through Anfield Cemetery. There would be a crowd of people walking to the match. No-one had cars, so there was a mass procession towards the ground.

My aunt lived in the shadow of Goodison Park but I did not like going there because she had a hairy face and she kissed me. Then you'd get 2s 6d. After the match we went back to my aunts' for a cup of tea, then to the pictures in Walton, followed by a fish and chip supper.

When I was older I went into the Boys' Pen. I loved the pushing and shoving. We never thought about dangers like Heysel and Hillsborough. Everyone seemed to have a flat cap and looked grey, in collar and tie. We did not have the world-wide knowledge of footie that young people have now. Today the rattles we used would be classed as dangerous. They were made of wood and plywood and painted Everton blue. Mum borrowed mine to go to a pensioners' fancy dress party recently. She went as an Everton supporter in shorts and a shirt. She still goes to the match, only now I take her. But she does not sit on my knee as I used to sit on her's when I was a child!

Michael Penn, born 1945

Jeans

My first pair of jeans were Wranglers, I was longing for a pair and my dad went out and got them at Flemings in Walton Road. My dad wore jeans because of his work in demolition so we knew how to make them soft. You put them in the bath with salt and soaked them. My sisters and I wore cheese-cloth shirts and trousers with big pockets. Toni Spencer was the place where you could buy lovely leather suits in beautiful colours. We bought clothes in St Johns precinct. I remember wearing a denim skirt buttoned down the front and shoes like sandals which laced up your legs. When I left school at seventeen, I went to work in Lewis' Food Hall. Little eighty-year-old ladies used to pinch the salmon and hide it in big pockets. Sometimes they got caught and were prosecuted. It was sad.

We used to go to the Silver Blades Ice Rink and skate to the music of the Bee Gees, David Essex, David Cassidy. We followed the fortunes of the ice rink team, The Leopards. I started smoking when I was sixteen. I had my first puff outside the rink and that was that. Drink never bothered me. I did not like the taste. I was one of six girls so, when I started my period my mother told me to go into her bedroom and get a towel but to make sure that my father never saw anything. I don't think my dad ever knew anyone had a period.

When we were small we played hopscotch and skipping and 'On the Mountain Stands a Lady.' My brother plugged his record player into the light socket in the back kitchen. I was the only one who could reach it. We went round the shops; Blacklers, Binns and especially Lewis' for a squirt of perfume.

Catherine Riley, born 1960

Ainsdale

Going to Ainsdale was always a treat. We would spend all day on the beach. If the sea was dirty it did not bother us. There were these terrible knitted swimming trunks which were a bit loose around the crotch. If you jumped in the water. you would lose them.

Michael Penn, born 1945

Lager

Lager was considered rather an exotic drink for students in the 1980s. Most girls did not drink anything but shandy or maybe wine. Liverpool pubs were

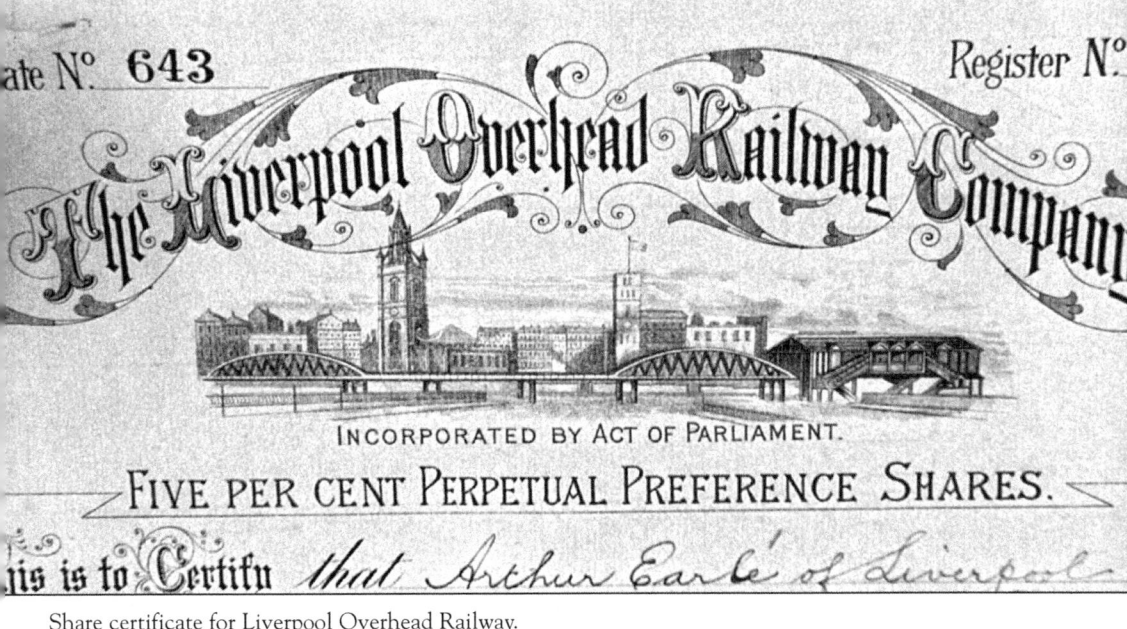

Share certificate for Liverpool Overhead Railway.

Doris Windsor (third from right) at Butlins, Pwllheli, 1949.

fairly down market and nightclubs were places where people went if they wanted to extend their drinking. There was no all-day drinking then. There was very little evidence of drugs, though there was always the whisper on the grapevine that someone might have some in their room.

David Owen, born 1966

Chelsea Girl

In the '80s if you had a Chelsea Girl bag you were the bee's knees. My first trainers were from the catalogue. I used to put my hair in curlers and wear plastic earrings.

Maria Ann Langan, born 1969

CHAPTER 4
Life and death

Doris Windsor (right) in Bangor with members of her family, 1937.

Babies

The midwife used to camp out in our house. Mother was always pregnant. She was having babies all the time. I was the eldest girl of eleven children. The boys did nothing or played cricket. The girls had to mind the children and take them shopping, so every time there was a new baby my face dropped. Our house was two-up and two-down. Dad slept in the back bedroom with the boys. Mother must have got pregnant while we were at Sunday school.

Doris Windsor, born 1917

Mrs McClean

Mrs McClean was one of the good women of the neighbourhood. She brought you into the world and sent you out. All babies were born at home and she used to arrive with the midwife. I was the eldest of seven and I was kept off school for a baby's birth. You could not go near the bedroom while mum was in labour. Until I was about thirteen I was naive and believed it when I was told that the baby was in the midwife's black bag. I wondered how it could breathe and she said the bag had little holes in it. Once I crept upstairs to see the baby come out of the bag but Mrs McClean opened the bedroom door and told me to get downstairs.

Molly Connor, born 1925

Birth Control

There was not much birth control in my mother's day. I was the eldest of nine children and was born when my

A group of children from Viola Street, 1962.

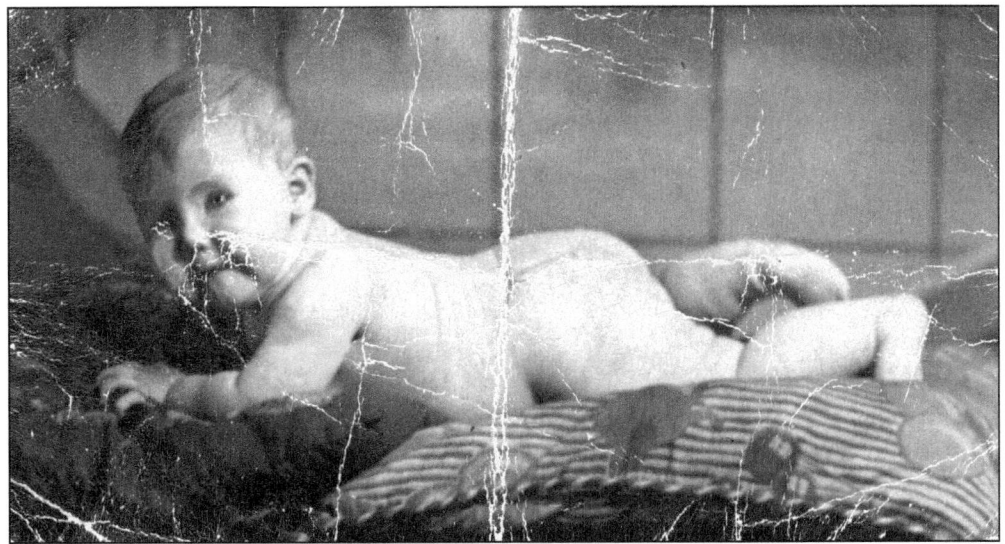
Vera Jeffers as a baby.

mother was nineteen. She had her last child when she was forty-three. She was not a Catholic.

Diana Dawson, born 1939

The Old Royal

The Liverpool Royal Infirmary was a teaching hospital and we had the cream of the medical profession. In 1946, I trained as a nurse there. I loved every minute of it. Miss Mary Jones had been appointed matron in 1935. She was a very remarkable woman; a strict disciplinarian. Though she was a diminutive figure her very presence in the hospital corridor produced a feeling of awe. We lived in at the Nurses Home and the only shock was that a lot of the girls had come into nursing to get away from home. I myself was very happy at home.

Ruth Halsall, born 1928

Baby Sitting

Mother used to go to Great Homer Street Market because it was cheaper. It was quite a way and dad went with her to carry things. I was left with the children: a three-week-old baby, one of two, one of four, one of eight, one of ten and a twelve year old. I had two in the bath and spilled boiling water. I did not know what to do. The child was screaming. I put flour on the burn which was probably the worst thing I could do.

When the doctor came he said the child would heal but it was me he was worried about. I should never have been left with that responsibility. Mother never put her arms round me. Perhaps she did not have time.

Doris Windsor, born 1917

Nursing

I always wanted to be a nurse. I'd get books with illustrations of fractures, out of Garston Library and draw them. When I signed up for my training in 1960 things were very formal. First year nurses wore striped collars, second year nurses Peter Pan collars and third years slim white collars – rather like a dog collar. Staff nurses had mauve uniforms, charge nurses, pale blue. In first, second and third year we had squares of white linen which covered all our hair. Then you got a cap we called a 'frillie' and which you made yourself.

Josephine Humphries, born 1942

Josephine Humphries proudly wears her 'frillie' nurse's cap.

The Wards

When I started at the old 'Royal' the corridors were wide and long. You almost needed a tram to get from one end to the other. In the outpatients' department there were narrow forms for the patients to sit on. Heating was by steam radiators and there were coal fires in the wards, The sluices where the bedpans were kept were freezing. Many of the wards were nightingale wards with high ceilings and a window between each bed. There were four round wards.

Things changed when the Salmon Report came in and a new structure of hospital management was introduced. Among other things matrons lost their titles. This was one thing that bothered me. I always felt a thrill being addressed as 'Nurse' or 'Sister'. I did not want to be called 'Miss'. The feeling of authority disappeared.

Ruth Halsall, born 1928

Leaving Home

Coming over from Ireland to train as a nurse meant leaving my family. I was seventeen and when I got off the boat I did not know what to do. But a wonderful taxi driver seemed to know exactly where I was going. He put my case in his cab and drove me straight to the nurses home. I could not get over how filthy and grimy Liverpool was. I looked up at the Liver Buildings and marvelled at the dirt.

Veronica McMahon, born 1932

Fever Hospital

When I was six I got diptheria. I know how I got it. I took water from the grid to make patacakes. I went to the Fever Hospital in a big red blanket and never saw my family for four months because I was isolated and infectious. My hair was cut short.

Ann Roberts, born 1937

Sefton General

Training to be a nurse at Sefton General was hard. There were quite a few Irish nurses there, but I was so lonely and homesick it was incredible. On the wards you did all the dirty work, bedpans, sluices. I can still remember the first person I saw die. He was called Mr Mountjoy. One minute he was there, the next he had gone. I will never forget the fright it gave me. He was so nice. You never get used to death but you learn to live with it, if you are a nurse. On the wards we worked from eight till eight. By then you were so tired all you did was have a bath and go straight to bed.

Veronica McMahon, born 1932

Fresh Air

The main treatment for TB when I was a child was fresh air. I had a strange, sickly childhood and spent a lot of time in hospital, after I was diagnosed with TB. There were classrooms where the windows used to fold down to create a flow of air. We

The window presented to the Liverpool Royal Infirmary in 1954, by the Nurses League.

had to have as much fresh air as possible.

Gerry Lipson, born 1929

Respect

The respect for consultants and doctors at the 'Royal' was tremendous and the patients were as much in awe of them as the nurses. You kept silent. Nobody dare speak. One ward sister liked the curtains between each bed drawn half way down before Lord Cohen did his rounds. Consultants drank ground coffee; the orderly sieved it through gauze. The white counterpanes on the bed all had Liver birds on them and the Liver birds had to be the right way up.

Josephine Humphries, born 1942

Delivering Babies

Midwifery training was hard work. You were in the Maternity Unit and then went out into the community. I was assigned to a midwife who had seen it all. You had to go out at night so I bought a bike and got a basket put on it, where I carried my medical bag. By that time the NHS was up and running but women had been used to paying the midwife. They saved sixpences in a jam jar. I was offered several such payments because the women thought they still had to pay. I never understood where this idea that there had to be towels and plenty of hot water came from. I had all I needed in my bag. But things have changed so much. We have epidurals. Now we have fathers at the birth which I think is wonderful. It gives them a chance of bonding sooner. They can change a baby's blood. My own son had this to make him into the fit, young man he is now. In days gone by, he would have died.

Veronica McMahon, born 1932

Former matron of Liverpool Royal Infirmary, Mary Jones pins the Gold Medal for achievement on Ruth Halsall, at the annual nurses prize-giving, 1949.

Calling The Doctor

It used to be 3s 6d to call the doctor out, 2s 6d if you went to see him. Once when my mother could not afford to call him, someone gave her a florin and she found 1s 6d from somewhere. People used home-made cures and things like Angers Emulsion.

Doris Windsor, born 1917

Home-made

There was a dispensary in Stanley Road. Doctors gave their time and you could get a cheap bottle of medicine there. Home-made remedies were used a lot. Camphor oil to rub the chest, cinnamon tea or vinegar for throats. If you were on the verge of bronchitis you used goose grease and brown paper. It worked every time.

Molly Connor, born 1925

Babies

There was never any sex education, so I did not know that when you were carrying a baby it was in a sack of water. It was my first child and I was only twenty. We had gone camping in Shropshire. Nine weeks before the baby was due, my waters broke but I did not know what was happening. People kept telling me it was a false alarm. But it was not.

It was love at first sight for my husband when we met at Queens Drive Baths. He was a keen cyclist and I had a sit up and beg bike which I had bought

Agnes Maddison with baby Paul, in Everton, 1957.

for 2s 6d a week from the catalogue. I was very proud of it. On our first ride I could not cycle home, so he gave me my bus fare and pushed my bike home for me.

When I got TB I was in hospital but my bed was out on a verandah, right into the winter. They put a rubber sheet over the bed when it snowed. I was so fed up I wrote to Clement Attlee and the Duke of Edinburgh telling them my husband had served in the Royal Navy, been awarded the Oak Leaf for gallantry after saving someone's life and been mentioned in despatches. They'd promised us a home fit for heroes yet we were living in terrible conditions and I was ill. The Duke of Edinburgh wrote

Princess Alexandra presents the prizes at the annual nurses prize giving of Liverpool Royal Infirmary, 1962.

back to say he could not interfere but would pass the letter on. This was about the same as I got from Mr Attlee. I don't know what happened but I came out of hospital to a council house in Croxteth. I loved it. There was a grassy slope which the kids used called Roly Poly. They would roll down it time and again. It kept them amused for hours.

Elizabeth Edwards, born 1929

Having Babies

There was picture on the ceiling of the hospital room where Professor Jeffcote examined me, when I was having trouble conceiving. It seemed nice. I did not realise it had been put there to take patients minds off the fact that they were being examined. We did everything correct: got engaged, got married in 1960. I thought, after that you had a baby. The girls in work were saving to get a house. All I wanted was a baby.

Mary Jenkins, born 1940

Crowded Conditions

In the south end of Liverpool around Upper Parliament Street, Toxteth and down to the Dingle there were a lot of Chinese and Nigerian families. Conditions were very crowded. One family where there were seven or eight children sat at the end of the bed and watched the baby arrive. The mother did not mind. But you did your best to give the woman in labour privacy. Considering the conditions in which people lived – no hot water, unless they boiled a kettle – their homes were spotless.

Veronica McMahon, born 1932

Infant Death

We were over the moon when I became pregnant but I was sick and could not keep my food down. They did not tell me that an X-ray had shown that the baby had no brain but they told my husband. When the child was born they said it was not quite right. I told them to put the child in an incubator but the doctor said 'No, your baby is dead.' It was terrible. The baby was a boy and I thought I would never get over it. I cannot remember asking where the baby was but I did not see him, nor did I bury the baby.

We had other children, then I became pregnant again. The child was overdue and had water on the brain. On the day I was coming out of hospital they asked if I could get in touch with an undertaker. It nearly killed me to think my child had been alone. They told me that with a stillborn baby you did not have a proper funeral. The undertaker said he would ask if the baby could be placed in a grave of someone else who was being buried. It was like penance to go and sit by the grave crying. My mother's grave was near and I knew, if she was looking down, she would be telling me not to be stupid and to go home.

Mary Jenkins, born 1940

Chinese Medicine

Being Chinese, my father did not like Western medicine. He would give us infusions made of dried leaves and flowers. They tasted foul. There was a herbalist shop in Nelson Street where you could get the ingredients he wanted. It always worked.

Susan Grainger, born 1948

Family Planning

In the '60s there was still need for family planning advice. I would give it whether they wanted it or not. The Irish were not too keen. In 1954 there was one woman who had five children, all with different dads.

Stillbirths are very traumatic. A woman has carried a child for nine months, and the baby has gone. Mothers in this situation need a lot of counselling. I could not cope with children dying.

Veronica McMahon, born 1932

Rheumatism

In the early days when I was nursing we saw a lot of rheumatic conditions. There was not the treatment there is now. Patients who came in with acute rheumatism were laid flat on their backs to keep their temperatures even, with their limbs wrapped in wadding, having been rubbed with liniment. There were gold injections for arthritis. The biggest medical and surgical changes has been the care of renal patients, which has given life and hope to so many in the way of dialysis and transplants.

Ruth Halsall, born 1928

Sex Education

Mum never talked about sex. If it came up you felt an atmosphere.

Maria Ann Langan, born 1969

Abortions

There were a lot of illegal abortions to deal with when I worked on the gynie ward, around 1952. Sometimes it seemed that every second woman who came in was an illegal abortion case. They were bleeding and suffering from an infection. There were plenty of back street abortionists about. Sometimes they tried to do it themselves and ended up in trouble. There were certainly those who came in habitually.

Veronica McMahon, born 1932

Contraception

The word sex was never mentioned by mum and dad. Mum thought the

Nurses from Liverpool Royal Infirmary, carol singing, Christmas, 1960.

word pregnant was rude. I had sisters and used to read their magazines. I learned a lot from them. My sisters learned about sex at school in biology with rabbits. There was an old joke that their headmistress would not allow them to wear patent leather shoes because you could see their knickers reflected in them.

Tom Eccleston, born 1948

Condoms

We were too embarrassed to ask for condoms. It was a case of pessaries and a wing and a prayer.

David Solomon, born 1916

No Pill

There was no Pill in my day. My mother told me nothing. I did not know what an abortion was until I was married.

Molly Connor, born 1925

The Birds and The Bees

You never talked about sex, though the lads whispered in each other's ears. Mother said we should always treat a lady with respect. You were lucky to get a kiss on the doorstep, never mind sex. In 1938 my auntie May was having a baby. We did not know what pregnant was.

Harry Mooney, born 1919

New Babies

Having babies was never mentioned. I remember my sister's new baby being put in a tomato basket. That was my nephew who became Archdeacon of London.

Lena Prince, born 1923

New Baby

Dad cried when he was knew I was pregnant. He had such high hopes for me. I was seventeen and had been going out with my boyfriend since I was fourteen. You did not know anything about sexually transmitted diseases then, and I thought if I did it once, I would not have to do it again. I was pregnant immediately and was hysterical. My boyfriend was terrified and my poor mum found out from someone else, who asked her if she had bought a hat for the wedding. Abortion was mentioned at the hospital but I could not do it: something to do with religion and taking a child's life.

The baby was born at Mill Road. It was the 1980s and the stigma had gone, but you could still see people peering at you as you walked down the road. My aunts and uncles said that it was not the end of the world and I was not the first. When I came home, I asked my dad if I could live with my boyfriend. After a week we decided to get married but in the end the marriage started to break up.

Joseph, my second child, was born with two holes in his heart and his main artery was open. I spent the next eleven months in the Childrens' Hospital, in

Herbert Massie and chums, Tweed Street, Liverpool 6, 1960.

Myrtle Street with him. But he died when he was eleven months old.

Catherine Riley, born 1960

Lime Street

The uniforms which English soldiers wore during the war were rough and hairy. I never went out with them. The Americans fetched you things off their ship. They would ask 'Do you or don't you?' I'd say 'No, I don't but if you want anyone, you can get up to Lime Street.'

Agnes Maddison, born 1927

Polio

When I contracted polio at the age of six months in the '50s there had been a big epidemic. They called it Infantile Paralysis. Some people were put in an iron lung machine with their head sticking out. I spent four and a half years in Alder Hey Hospital. When I finally went home at the age of five, it was a whole new world. I was astonished that rooms could be so small. I was used to huge hospital wards.

Herbert Massie, born 1949

TB

They had a special block for TB patients in Walton Hospital. I went there in 1950, when I was diagnosed as having tuberculosis. My son John was fourteen months old and my mother looked after him. When I coughed, my hanky was bloodstained. The treatment was to put a needle under your diaphragm and pump air in. By screening they could tell how much air you had taken it. The idea was to compress your lung and rest it so that it would heal. I was in hospital for eighteen months. There were no drugs for TB then. You had to stay in bed and get your weight up. Then you were allowed up for one hour a day, increasing to eight hours, when they let you go home for a week. You were warned not to come back pregnant.

Vera Jeffers, born 1925

Engaged

I was married in 1964, but when I got engaged Sister Haynes told me to put my ring on a thread and hang it round my neck. She said it would be much nearer my heart.

Josephine Humphries, born 1942

Biology

There was no sex education at St Francis Xaviers. We did biology lessons and learned from books and other boys.

John McEwan, born 1939

Gays

Homosexuals and lesbians did attract snide jokes. We called them 'homos' not 'gays'. To my knowledge I did not know any when I was young.

John McEwan, born 1939

Same Sex

Homosexuals I knew nothing about until I met two at the Silver Blades Ice Rink. They were great guys and one was my friend's brother. She explained it to me.

I was not shocked but I thought it was different.

Catherine Riley, born 1960

Contraception

I fell in love from the word go and we got engaged after four years, coming up to my twenty-first birthday. We did our courting in the front room and eventually I plucked up courage and told my mum I wanted to go on the Pill. She said 'Okay, do you want me to come with you?' We got married in 1990.

Maria Ann Langan, born 1969

Disabled

Though I was on crutches after polio, my family made no allowances for my disability. If they played football, I was the goalkeeper. My father was determined that I would be independent. He put two ropes down as parallel bars to help me walk. It was the days of street gangs when young people were very territorial. If there were any fights my friends would push me to one side and see that I got home okay. I had five different operations in connection with my polio. None of them did me any good. I developed the idea we were

Herbert Massie taking the sun in the Caribbean.

being used as guinea pigs.

Herbert Massie, born 1949

Home Helps

A lot of the elderly have no family; if you are a home help, as I was, you can walk into a house where someone is sitting crying because they are so fed up. So before you do the shopping and the cleaning you have to deal with that. Some are in wheelchairs, others you have to clean them as they come off the commode. Home helps do not get the rewards and recognition they deserve.

Catherine Riley, born 1960

Charity

As far as the disabled are concerned, the Royal Association for Disability and Rehabilitation, a charity which I joined in 1978, goes back to 1919 and has been the most successful organisation for campaigning on behalf of them. We have not gone in for demonstrations in a big way. We operate behind the scenes. From 1 January 1999, every new train has to have facilities for disabled passengers – that includes toilet facilities. Liverpool, I am proud to say, introduced the first wheelchair accessibility buses on public routes in the country. Interestingly some Tory ministers fought hard for it, yet some left wing ministers, well known politicians behind the scenes, opposed everything and now take credit for it.

Herbert Massie, born 1949

Death

My mother had asthma and TB. She was always upstairs in bed, if you could not find her by the stove or the fire. She was forty-four the day she died. My mam's friend Queenie sent me to get some milk and I knew to wait round the corner because the ambulance would be coming. One of my friend's sisters was getting married at the Sacred Heart Church in Hall Lane, and we were collecting the confetti. I said I would have to go home because it was nearly dinner time and she said it was no good me going home because my mam was dead. I set about her, for telling lies but I remember the feeling at the pit of my stomach, the fear of going home. I was used to her being in hospital, but it was

Ann Roberts' mother, Ann Rafferty.

Ann Roberts aged one.

comforting that she was around. When I got home my dad was sitting at the table with his head in his hands. I was told not to upset him.

Ann Roberts, born 1937

Undertaker

My dad was an undertaker. A wake could go on for three days. There was a lot of drink. It was an excuse for a knees-up. You paid sixpence to take a jug of ale home. I once saw an old lady who had died, with pennies on her eyes and a saucer of salt on her chest. Don't ask me why. When dad went to a party, he used to stand behind people with a tape measure in his hand. He had a good sense of humour.

Agnes Maddison, born 1927

The Hearse

Though we had always been involved in transport going back to the days of hansom cabs, in 1933 my father realised that people in south Liverpool were going to buy their own cars. He decided to diversify and had a hearse body built onto an old Daimler. Other firms like Charlettes and F.A Collinsons of Smithdown Road started down the same route. Then, when people died, the bodies would lie in the house for three or four days and friends came to pay their respects. Fewer people were cremated then. After the National Heath Service began people started to die in hospital, so father built a little Chapel of Rest. Some funerals were more lively than others. People could get into fisticuffs. It was nothing for them to start drinking at eight o'clock in the morning on the day of the funeral.

Patrick Pearson, born 1933

Respect

The day of my mother's funeral, I remember the street lined with neighbours. You saw people doffing their caps or crossing themselves. My dad died four years later and my sister came to school to get me. Next day the nuns came to the door and said 'We are taking Anne to the convent.' My sister Gwen said 'You are taking her nowhere.' My grandad said 'No-one goes into a home from this family.'

Ann Roberts, born 1937

CHAPTER 5

Beliefs, fears, justice and injustice

The Pope at prayer in Liverpool Metropolitan Cathedral, 1982. Archbishop Derek Worlock is on the left and Cardinal Basil Hume, on the right.

Religious Politics

As the older generation will remember, years ago the political element between Catholics and Protestants was very much stronger than now. Every year on 12 July when the Orange Lodge marched there was trouble. The divisions were strict. Some firms would not employ Catholics.

Father Denis McDonnell, born 1907

Trouble

On 12 July grass sods used to be thrown at the Orange Lodge procession. My mother would call me in and tell me not to get involved. St Francis Xavier Roman Catholic School, where I went was just a stone's throw from the Protestant Liverpool Collegiate but there was never any problem as far as I was aware.

John McEwan, born 1939

Heaven

You were taught that only Catholics went to Heaven and if you told a lie your tongue would turn black.

Agnes Maddison, born 1927

C of E

We were non-Conformist but I went to a Church of England school where we got religion rammed down our throats. As I was a good reader I was asked to read aloud each day. I thought it was a load of tripe. Some of the parables were awful, though I do believe there was a man called Jesus; a Socialist ahead of his time. I used to kneel at the end of the bed and pray but my mind was on how many sausages there were in the fridge. It was a case of the working class being kept down and told that though they were getting rotten wages there was a mansion waiting in Heaven.

Doris Windsor, born 1917

Early Mass

Religion was central to my family. It sounds incredibly pious but I went to church to serve mass at seven o'clock in the morning every day before going to school. I went into the seminary when I was fourteen and was ordained at twenty-four. In those ten years I would guess that ninety per cent of young men would leave.

Father Michael Gaine, born 1930

Lloyd George

Catholics suffered desperately and unfairly from lack of education. But the Archbishops were prepared to fight for it. At one time Archbishop Whiteside told Lloyd George that if necessary he would put every child in Liverpool out on the street by way of protest. He, like Archbishop Downey, could call all Liverpool out on the streets with a snap of his fingers, whether they went to Mass or not. But the education came and the first Catholic teacher

Father Michael Gaine (right) at the ordination of his brother John at Upholland Seminary, 1951.

training schemes were established. The teachers, being nuns, worked for nothing.

Father Denis McDonnell, born 1907

Best Clothes

Religion was very important in my family. We wore our best clothes on Sunday and polished our shoes. Liverpool 8 was very much an Orange Lodge area. All the houses were decorated on 12 July. As a child I would love to have taken part in the Orange Lodge procession and been Queen Mary or King Billy waving my sword about. We used to say the Orange Lodge had prayer books with handles, meaning they were always in the pubs.

Lena Prince, born 1923

Influence

Though Catholics with money had influence, the Church in Liverpool was very much Labour.

Father Denis McDonnell, born 1907

Two Sorts of Catholics

There was a large community of Catholics in Liverpool, who were largely of Irish descent. There were other Catholics on the outskirts of Liverpool and in Lancashire, including the old aristocratic families. This made for two quite different sorts of Catholics in the north west.

Father Michael Gaine, born 1930

Ecumenism

There was no sense of ecumenism in Liverpool when I was growing up. A Church of England girl could not be a bridesmaid to a friend who was a Roman Catholic. As a Protestant I was very aware of their being a real split between what Catholics did and what we did. I don't think either side wanted ecumenism. That did not come until the Roman Catholic Archbishop Worlock and David Sheppard, the Anglican Bishop started working together, over twenty years ago. They did so much for the under privileged, marching for the unemployed, looking for jobs and better housing. They also started the Pentecostal Walks. One year they would begin at the Metropolitan Cathedral and walk to the Anglican Cathedral to sing and pray. Next year the walk would start at the Anglican Cathedral and make its way to the Metropolitan Cathedral. There was barracking from the Orange Lodge.

Lena Prince, born 1923.

Ridicule

Girls married young – at seventeen or eighteen. Boys when they left school stopped going to Mass because they were getting ridiculed. You did not worry because when they married the girls would bring them back.

Father Denis McDonnell, born 1907

Lena Prince and other women priests await their ordination by the Bishop of Liverpool, David Sheppard at Liverpool Cathedral in 1994.

Robert Runcie, the Archbishop of Canterbury kneels in prayer at Liverpool parish church, when members of the Orange Lodge protested against the Pope's visit to Liverpool, in 1982.

Peter's Purse

Catholics used to talk about the priest coming round and families having money ready on the sideboard. They called it Peter's Purse. They would give their last pennies but I thought it was wrong for the Church to take the money meant for the children's food. Many families were very, very poor. We went to our church and took our collection, a penny or whatever it was.

Lena Prince, born 1923

Big Day

My mother was a true Christian who would never see anyone down. She was a member of the Royal Orange Institution of England and 12 July was her big day. It was lovely to see her in her white and orange sash. It was the only holiday she took. Mind you it was very unusual for anyone to have a holiday. On 12 July, Dolly the pony used to carry the queen on her back. I don't remember trouble except sometimes in London Road.

Harry Mooney, born 1919

Spoilt Priest

Anyone who entered a seminary and left had the label 'spoilt priest' around his neck for life. Many did leave, for right and proper reasons.

Father Michael Gaine, born 1930

The Ministry

I was round about eighteen when my spiritual life was born and I knew I had a growing vocation. I wanted to train for the Ministry. In 1960 I started in the Church as a lay person and was allowed to read the Lesson. Big deal. By 1966 I was a deaconess which then was still the only form of Ministry open to women. As deaconess I thought it was as far as I could go and felt frustrated, though I had to work within the rules. I was fairly militant and campaigned for the ordination of women in the Church of England but I never thought it would come in my time. But I knew there were all these women coming up behind me and I had to fight for them.

Women's ordination finally arrived and I was the first of ninety-four women priests to be ordained in Liverpool Cathedral by Bishop David Sheppard in May 1994. The day itself was quite wonderful. Never in my wildest dreams did I ever think that I would become a priest in the Church of England. I thought back to all the people who had helped me along the way. There had been a lot of opposition and there are still those who are discourteous. I have not experienced it much myself, except for one lady who left instructions that I was not to conduct her funeral.

Lena Prince, born 1923

John (Brian) Griffin's first Holy Communion Certificate.

Barbara Phythian's mother and uncle, Edith and Alfred Hindle, when children in 1910.

The 'Boss'

In the old days, the parish priest was the boss and you obeyed him though you called him for everything. People were afraid of him, he was very much in control. If you coughed while he was speaking in the pulpit, he stopped and waited for half a minute, You could hear a pin drop.

Father Denis McDonnell, born 1907

Sickened

By the age of fifteen, I had had a sickener of church. Before that I went twice on Sunday. My sister wanted to marry a non-Catholic and wished to do so before the main altar – every girl's dream. Her husband-to-be went for instruction for thirteen weeks because he wanted to change to Catholicism. If you were marrying a non-Catholic you were married at the side altar. In the end my sister was married in the vestry. She might as well have gone up to Brougham Terrace Register Office. The Monsigner told her she had no business marrying someone who was not a Catholic.

Ann Roberts, born 1937

Mixed Marriages

Mixed marriages were treated as almost undesirable and did not take place at the High Altar of the church. It was an incredibly insensitive way of dealing with something which was fundamental to a family.

Father Michael Gaine, born 1930

Tory Voter

I used to think Catholic children should be ashamed because they were Catholic. Dad leaned towards the Orange Lodge and always voted Tory, even though he had not got a penny.

Doris Windsor, born 1917

Church Collection

The priest visited every house and pub in his parish. The money was for the church upkeep. Sixpence was the going rate. The Church never had any shortage of money. There was loads of it. In the 1950s there were two or three priests in each parish.

You had to be back in the house by ten o'clock otherwise you would find the doors locked.

I knew I would enter the priesthood when I was eleven or twelve. My father and I were going for a walk and he said 'Would you like to be a priest?' I said 'Yes' and the matter was never raised again. I went to a seminary in Waterford when I was eighteen and did my theology at Upholland where I was ordained in 1929. My first parish was at St Sebastians in Fairfield and I've never been out of Liverpool since.

Father Denis McDonnell, born 1907

12 July

In Great Homer Street we lived in the heartland of the Orange Lodge. On 12 July the Protestants used to wait for you and throw stones. But it was only school kids. There were barricades like you see in Northern Ireland now. But the violence they talk about on Scottie Road and Great Homer Street was nothing compared to today. You could walk home from the pictures in the dark.

Molly Connor, born 1925

Privilege

When I was thirteen or fourteen, I was allowed to clean behind the altar. It was a great privilege. I firmly believed that God was in that Tabernacle. If I touched the curtain while I washed the marble I used to say 'Sorry, God.' In particular my grandma Rafferty was very devout. She had a white cat called Beulah. The cat would sit with the fire roaring up the chimney. It was scorched all down one side.

Ann Roberts, born 1937

King Billy

Mother was Protestant and dad Catholic but mum converted. When the Orange Lodge walked up the road we'd sing 'We'll hang King Billy from the sour apple tree' and they'd sing 'Down with Popery.' If you had Catholic neighbours you only fell out for one day – 12 July.

Agnes Maddison, born 1927

Divide

As a child I was aware of the Catholic-Protestant divide, though we had no problem with religion. I loved the Lodge marches because they were on my birthday.

The nuns at school were very strict. When we started wearing bobby sox, Mother Margaret sent for us and asked if it was some sort of cult or gang and told us we would end up in prison.

Mary Jenkins, born 1940

Altar Boy

We were a religious family and from the age of six, I served on the altar at the Church of Our Lady in Eldon Street. I learned the Latin Mass till I was fifteen and I would get up and serve Mass at seven o'clock in the morning. There were four priests. On Wednesday there was a novena to Our Lady. The first bell would go at seven o'clock and we would be playing football in Eldon Grove. The second bell went at quarter past seven, and we stopped playing football and ran like ruddy hell to get washed and into our cassocks. The priest would look at your hands and turn them over and they would be dirty on the back. I thought I might as well have stayed playing football. Then you would get a belt round the ear for not getting washed properly.

Your parents had to buy your cassock. If it was getting short, the priest could see your black pumps. Or you might have boots on because you had been playing football. You often wore boots or wellies. Anyone who had a pair of pumps to play football was well off. If you left your pumps in the Presbytery, someone who did not have any, would

The Clay family: Joyce, Kay, Diana and Ron in Vale Park, New Brighton, 1947.

wear them. At other times I did messages for the priests and got the coal from the cellar for the equivalent of 70p a week.

Jim Wafer, born 1944

Throwing Bottles

In the '50s we used to go and watch the Orange Lodge walking in procession to Exchange Station, where they got on the train to Southport. Sometimes people threw bottles. I remember one occasion when the band was passing down Moorfields and the man playing the drum, simply put it down and went into a pub.
Strangely enough when I got my first posting as a Probation Officer in 1972, the office was between Scotland Road and Netherfield Road, the Catholic-Protestant divide.

Michel Penn, born 1945

Friendships

We were a Jewish family but I formed great friendships at West Kirby High School with non-Jewish boys, particularly with one of the Gordon family, who were pawnbrokers and well known around Liverpool. I was never aware of any real anti-Semitism but we had a billiard table and I did notice that he came to my house more than I went to his. I did feel there was something.

David Solomon, born 1916

Gospel Choir

After the war a man called Pastor Daniels ran a gospel choir in Hill Street. He let off rooms to anyone who was poor and had a nursery, with cots, for babies whose fathers had been black Yanks and had gone back to America. He wanted to get people off the street and would try and help them. He used to serve hot cocoa.

Charles Jenkins, born 1937

Cardinal Heenan

Cardinal Heenan who succeeded Archbishop Godfrey as Archbishop of Liverpool in 1957 and followed him to Westminster, was one of Liverpool's more active Bishops – a man going places. He

Rome, 1957 and Father Michael Gaine is pictured with Pope Pius XII and Archbishop William Godfrey, Archbishop of Liverpool, to whom he was secretary.

was a diplomat and a politician and had published a book *The Peoples Priest*. His central idea was that the priest was there for the people, not them for him. He had an obligation to care for them, no matter what the cost.

In the late 1950s he bullied the government into establishing a Catholic grammar school. Religious bigotry was deeply rooted. There was a legal battle against Catholics being able to purchase the old workhouse site on which to build the Catholic cathedral. Alderman Longbottom (leader of the Protestant Party on Liverpool City Council) was on record as saying that he would sooner have a germ factory on Brownlow Hill than a Catholic cathedral. It sounds funny with hindsight, but it was bitterly and seriously meant.

Father Michael Gaine, born 1930

Alderman the Revd H.D. Longbottom, Leader of the Protestant Party on Liverpool City Council.

Confession

I hated going to confession because I was frightened of it. I used to struggle to find things to say.

Maria Ann Langan, born 1969

Communion

I do not go to confession all the time, but I take Communion even though I am divorced, which would annoy some people. I do love my faith, but there are things I can take and things I can leave. I believe in ecumenism.

Catherine Riley, born 1960

Faith

I do not have a faith, but I would like one. I used to think I would like to be Jewish, because of the emphasis on family life.

Anne Williams, born 1939

Education

Father was very religious and when I was eleven he decided that I should go to a Jewish school in Cambridge, founded in 1603. It's still going. When I was thirteen he thought I was not getting sufficient Jewish education so I went to Birkenhead School. I was not particularly bright – middle of the class.

David Solomon, born 1916

Archbishop Derek Worlock and David Sheppard, Anglican Bishop of Liverpool, who led the ecumenical movement.

Notepaper

Cardinal Heenan had special notepaper, roughly the size of a postcard. He'd write two sentences: 'By all means. God bless you.'

Father Michael Gaine, born 1930

Ecumenism

Within a year of David Sheppard becoming the Anglican Bishop of Liverpool, in 1975, Derek Worlock was appointed as the Roman Catholic Archbishop. The day he arrived, David Sheppard called at his house with a bottle of wine. They quickly became friends. Both were keen on ecumenism. I think the political initiative came from David Sheppard initially. He was already an evangelist and Socialist in thinking. He'd written books on the problems of city life. The two of them educated each other. Very quickly they were meeting regularly and phoning each other every day. They exchanged dates in their diaries so that they did not clash. I suppose you could say it was quite revolutionary. Ecumenism became more evident.

They decided that they needed the Free Church tradition so the Church leaders became a threesome. But everyone was more interested in David Sheppard and Derek Worlock and they found that the Free Church man would be cut off photographs. They made sure this did not happen by standing him in the middle. They set a pattern; they did everything together. They were involved with the Toxteth Riots in 1981, they built bridges with Ken Oxford the Chief Constable. They helped set up the Liverpoool 8 Law Centre.

The Sheppard-Worlock partnership was an historic milestone. The two of them made a great amalgam. Perhaps one could see it at its height when Militant were in charge of Liverpool. But I do not think that the pattern of ecumenism will occur again. It is not necessary for all three churches to be a platform together.

Father Michael Gaine, born 1930

Gay Priests

The problem of the ordination of homosexuals in the Church of England is a difficult one, but I believe being homosexual is something you are born with. Therefore I don't mind a gay priest or a lesbian being ordained as long as their relationship is as strict as a heterosexual's; and they do not go shopping around. They must be faithful and love one another.

Lena Prince, born 1923

Tridentine Mass

When the Vatican moved away from the Latin Mass, and after three hundred and fifty years the Tridentine Mass died on the vine, the rebel Archbishop Le Febre opened a church in Edge Lane where it could be celebrated. Archbishop Worlock did not want to give Catholics the excuse of saying there was no official Tridentine Mass in Liverpool, so he asked me if I would say it at my church, St Mary's, Highfield in the city. I found it psychologically difficult because I preferred the style of the new vernacular mass. It brought with it an appreciation of the liturgy but the Tridentine Mass does have something in the way of solemnity.

Father Michael Gaine, born 1930

Masons

People have got the wrong idea about Masons. The suggestion that we are very clannish and only protect and defend one another is a lot of twaddle. The masons do a lot of good work very quietly and very charitably. Especially among the very poor. There is nothing devious or nasty about anyone being a mason.

Gerry Lipson, born 1929

Married Clergy

A priest who is married with a child is a plus in today's world, in my view.

Lena Prince, born 1923

South Liverpool

There are a lot of Jewish people in South Liverpool and my family are very proudly Jewish. I have always been associated with Harold House. the Jewish Youth Club, which has done so much and where I am a trustee.

Gerry Lipson, born 1929

Women's Lib

The fact that women had to put up with inequality was obvious to me when I was young. In the late '70s when Women's Lib came in, I was already a Women's Libber. In fact, my second husband used to say I was a Women's Libber before anyone.

Diana Dawson, born 1939

Wage Packet

Believe it or not, I had to hand my wage packet to my husband unopened. One of his favourite words was 'allow'. He would say 'I cannot allow this.' Or 'I cannot allow that.'

Elizabeth Edwards, born 1929

Ramblers

You have to fight for what you believe in. One of the reasons I joined the Ramblers in 1983 was because my dog had died and I wanted an excuse to get out into the fresh air. I love the countryside and am very much involved with the access problem and the right to roam. We do not just want to walk up a hill one way and down another. Everyone deserves to be able to enjoy the countryside, but the landowners do not agree.

Most of the Trough of Bowland belongs to the Duke of Westminster and he seems to think it is his back garden. There, men will pay £10,000 a day to shoot birds. They are doing it four days a week, so no wonder the land owners are not keen on ramblers. There is a lot of Britain's country closed off to ordinary people, like the Trough of Bowland. This, incidentally is one of the Queen's favourite places. She said if she could retire that is where she would go. What is not understood by the landowners is that most ramblers are decent, respectable people, not a lot of yobs.

Diana Dawson, born 1939

Mother

It was the sight of my mother looking gaunt and drained when I had got into trouble with the police and was in court, which really pulled me up sharp. Something ripped inside me and I swore that I would not get into trouble again. A similar thing happened when I was twenty-seven and knew I had a daughter on the way: I gave up smoking cannabis which I had been doing since I was a lad. I watched the birth of my daughter and when I held her and looked down at her, my inside turned over.

Gerald Clarkson, born 1967

Single Mum

More and more men are taking a child care role, though ninety-one per cent of single parent families are female. Abortion was never an option when I found I was pregnant. I was twenty-five and I felt no shame. In the '80s I was clubbing it, going to Kirklands. I had money and would

Agnes Maddison and new husband Norman cut the cake after their wedding at St Johns, Kirkdale, 1951.

spend £55 on a shirt at Next. Things changed when I was expecting the baby. At nine weeks old I took her with me to the NNEB nursery course I was doing. I used to feed her during lectures and hand in exam papers smudged with breast milk.

Karen Chasen, born 1969

Single Dad

When my partner agreed to me having custody of our daughter, when we split, I was glad; though it is hard work being a single parent, while doing a degree. But with help and advice from the Liverpool One Parent Trust, I can cope. I am capable. My life is college – and my daughter.

Gerald Clarkson, born 1967

Probation Service

It was through helping out at West Derby Youth Club that I went into the Probation Service, One of the youth leaders who was a probation officer himself, told me he thought I would be good at it. The first day in the job, I was frightened to death. My first client lived in Roscommon Street and was about seventeen. I wrote to him and told him to come in, but he did not, so I went to the house and banged on the door. He ran out and soft lad here ran after him. I learned afterwards that it was not how you behaved.

Initially prisons were quite brutal. There was little in the way of rehabilitation, education and job training. People were numbers, not human beings, They were not allowed contact with their families. Visiting was once a month for half an hour. There was an expectancy they would come out better people, but the investment was not there. The thinking was that these people had offended against society and should be locked away.

Very often they came out of prison worse than when they went in. They had lost their jobs and their families had broken up. All they would emerge with would be a grant, a bag of clothing and little else. Nothing had been done in the development of the Probation Service, but then a more constructive attitude did develop. It was realised that you could not expect people to walk out of prison and back into society as if nothing had happened. It was not surprising that they kept going back again.

The nature of offending against the law has changed. What people will do to get money has changed. Years ago men would not do shop lifting. That was a woman's crime. They would not go into Marks and Spencer and pinch something. Nowadays it is an easy way of getting £20 for a fix. There is a lot of prostitution, rent boys and young girls but working class people will not do it near where they live. Drugs are not related to class. There are more women around with access to alcohol and drugs. They have adopted male roles. There are girls gangs.

Michael Penn, born 1945

CHAPTER 6
Food and drink

A Festival of Britain gathering, 1951. Molly Connor is on the front row, second from right.

Coopers

Coopers in Church Street was the Harrods Food Hall of Liverpool and to walk in and ask if you could work there would have been like approaching Al Fayed. One day, my uncle, who was the Chief Clerk at the Magistrates Court said 'Would you like to work at Coopers?' I said 'Yes, it will be a job.' He said 'No, it will be more than that because if I get you in there you will be an apprentice buyer.' I put on my best suit and went down to Coopers where my uncle introduced me to Bertram Chrimes who was the managing director, and Mr Molyneux, the general manager. They took me on.

Coopers had its own smell which attracted everyone. There was a lovely atmosphere as you walked through the beautiful Victorian glass doors. As you stepped inside there were tiled floors. There was a commissioner in nice green livery. All the counter staff wore grey and the floor managers frock coats. It was like *Are You Being Served?*

Someone well known and well up would probably arrive in a car which drew up outside the shop. You'd go to them, bring them in and walk them over to the grocery counter and draw up a chair for them to sit down. Someone would say 'Harris, look after Mrs S.' That was my customer for whatever she wanted. She would wish to have an order made up and I would escort her to other counters and her order would go down to the basement. It would be put into a strong basket and delivered to her house. If she was taking it with her I would parcel it up and take it to the car.

Arthur Harris, born 1919

Christmas

There were usually twenty-five for Christmas lunch. There was a double range at the Dock Master's House where we lived. Mother would have a piece of ham in one oven, a piece of pork in another and the turkey turning on a spit. One of the skippers of a ship from Oporto, brought a glass box with muscatels wrapped in tissue. Dad would get presents of bottles of brandy and wine. We never lacked for fresh fish. There was a zinc bath where you would find everything from conger eel to delicate sole. A piece of salt ling would be hung in the cellar and each Saturday you'd cut a piece off and put it to soak, ready for Sunday morning.

Madge Parry, born 1899

Supermarkets

The first supermarket I remember was Tesco's in Moor Lane. It was nice to compare prices. You felt in control. There were packet soups: things you had never seen before.

Agnes Maddison, born 1927

Food

In the 1930s when money was tight, I used to go across to a neighbour who made chips, which we'd buy. I'd take a bowl over to her house. There was another woman who made iced cakes and sold them by the dozen. It was cheaper than the shops. My mother got help from the Church. There were vouchers you could take to a shop and get 5s worth of groceries or other food.

When food rationing came, there was a little black market went on. People stopped taking sugar. It was marvellous what people could do with almost nothing. I'd go round to my fiancé's sister and she would break an egg and whip it up, put bread in it and fry it. Then put jam on it. Tasty little things made out of nothing.

Vera Jeffers, born 1925

No Fridges

In the days when there were no fridges, people shopped every day. After six, they auctioned the meat off in Great Homer Street. The women in the markets wore long skirts, with boots and men's socks and shawls. The posh wore very heavy shawls. I heard they used to boil oranges to make them shiny. I don't know if that was true.

Agnes Maddison, born 1927

Coffee

They used to roast the coffee upstairs in Coopers. There was a special sugar room. Everything was sold loose. Customers knew what they wanted whether it was Darjeeling tea or Orange Pekoe, or a bag of first grade sultanas. Bananas would come from the docks green, and the 'hands' were hung in rows in a special room. The fruit and vegetable department would ring up when they needed some which were ripe.

At one point I was on the dog food department so I knew all the different dog biscuits. One Christmas I was put into the wine department to make up orders. That was when I realised there were different grades of champagne. Coopers was a lovely place to work. I learned a lot. I could still cut you a pound of butter with a couple of butter pats.

Arthur Harris, born 1919

Blind Scouse

My mother used to make scouse. When it contained no meat, it was called blind scouse. Sometimes I'd be sent to the corner shop to get a cup

Trooper Arthur Harris in the uniform of the Duke of Lancaster's Yeomanry, 1938.

John Griffin, when a small boy.

of jam. You'd put the cup on the scales to be weighed. Then it would be filled with jam and weighed again. You were charged for the jam. We got our groceries from the Maypole. They were wrapped in brown paper and tied with string. The butter was shaped with butter pats.

Lena Prince, born 1923

Well Fed

I can't say we were poor. We fed well. Bacon and eggs, porridge every day. Mother always cooked a leg of lamb at the weekend for Sunday lunch. We had it cold on Sunday night and in some sort of hash on Monday. There was no Italian food or Chinese. We used to buy chips and ask for the chip scrap pieces which had fallen into the fat. There was a plain wooden form where you sat and waited to be served. When we had a party mum borrowed it.

John Griffin, born 1931

Sensible

Growing up in the '20s and '30s we did not know about poverty, but we ate sensibly. There was none of this throwing cream and red wine into things. We had roast beef and Yorkshire pudding, steamed puddings with lovely custard. Rice pudding. We did not worry about fat. Father always had his whisky and soda and cigar at night. I had a little taste of sherry and did not like it. Mother had these wonderful tea parties. There was Mrs Owen, the bank manager's wife, Mr Dawson, the solicitor, Mrs Markham the vicar's wife and the accountant's wife. I remember there was always a cake stand. The first Chinese restaurant we went to was up these filthy steps. We thought it was wonderful.

Joan Wyn-William, born 1910

Plain Food

My mother loved tripe. She used to stew it in milk. She also bought pigs' trotters or half a pig's head. She would shave the hairs off it and put it in a pan. Plain food did not do us any harm.

Jack Lindo, born 1919

Scouse

We lived on scouse. I loved bacon ribs and tripe. The butcher had a big barrel by the door where he put all sorts of bits and pieces in vinegar. Mum used to take out pig's feet. It sounds awful, but take it from me, there was some good stuff in there. Even oxtail sometimes. We never had a salad. If you had an apple you were rich.

George Armstrong, born 1929

Bread and Jam

There were no school dinners when I was at school. You could have Horlicks, but we could not afford it. You went home for lunch which was usually scouse and I did not like. You never had 'afters'. There was bread and jam for tea but Sunday dinner was always good. Pineapple chunks were a treat. For some reason the Christmas oranges seemed sour.

Doris Windsor, born 1917

Rice Pudding

Food was very basic. We did not have a varied menu. I used to hate rice pudding. The thought of that skin! Later I'd do anything to have that lovely skin on the rice pudding which to my mind is always sweet.

Gerry Lipson, born 1929

Free Dinners

If your dad was not working you got free dinners at Chalmers Hall in Westminster Road. We also got free clothes from some organisation. I am not ashamed to say that.

George Armstrong, born 1929

Wedding Breakfast

When I married my first husband in 1940, we had York ham and salad, sherry trifle and fresh pastries. It cost 2s 9d a head.

Doris Windsor, born 1917

Meal Time

Meals were eaten in dribs and drabs though on Sunday we all sat down together. Scouse was made out of anything cheap; four pennyworth of scrag end and two and a half pound of potatoes for two pence. Two pennyworth of mixed veg would be thrown in.

Jack Lindo, born 1919

On The Farm

We came to Ledsham in 1909 and when I was eighteen I started working on the farm. We had twenty-six acres at first and were milking twenty cows. We kept pigs for butchery purposes. I plucked geese and mother took them to market in Liverpool. She

Festival of Britain street party, Tillard Street, 1951.

made cheese and I used to stir the blood from the pigs to make black pudding. As a child I looked for plovers eggs. Mother would take them to market and sell them for 1s each.

In the 1930s we were delivering milk from our farm in Ledsham, in the south end of Liverpool. We took the milk over on the boat. You drove up the floating roadway, which rose and fell with the tide. The Mersey Tunnel made a big difference.

Joseph Wilson, born 1914

Pigeon Pie

Pigeon pie was a treat. My uncle Nelson who lived in Walton used to have pigeons, so sometimes we'd have pigeon pie. We caught pigeons at a church in Great Homer Street with a piece of cotton. You tempted them with bread and lassooed their foot.

George Armstrong, born 1929

Getting By

Before there was such a thing as Social Security people had to scrounge and scrape to get by. You did without or starved.

Jack Lindo, born 1919

Chanticleer

Mum and dad liked Chinese food. When I was a kid, they went to the Chanticleer, one of the few Chinese restaurants around then. The big one was the Far East. Mum was having a Chinese meal when she went into labour with my little sister. She was taken to hospital. When I looked at the baby in her cot, I thought she had slitty eyes and I remember wondering, whether this was because my mother had so many Chinese meals.

Michael Penn, born 1945

Drinks Licence

Up until 1961, Coopers in Church Street could not sell alcoholic drinks in the restaurant. Then they made an application for a drink's licence, to Liverpool Magistrates. When

Arthur McFarland, who was the stipendiary magistrate, and lunched there regularly, heard about this he said he would never go there for lunch again if they got it. They did.

Arthur Schmuhl, born 1916

Licensees

Pub licensees were expected to be of exemplary behaviour. When my dad was applying for a licence, he was worried he would not get it because as a boy, he had been caught playing football in the street and fined.

After thirty years working in pubs, I can tell you how things have changed. When opening hours were stricter, you had men with several pints lined up in front of them when closing time came. There was one man we called four-pint Stan. He'd arrive in the pub at about ten minutes to ten and you could not get rid of him. My dad used to ask him if he could not drink a bit quicker. Sometimes the police came. They were always in twos and they were looking for underage drinkers and making sure there was no singing.

People drank beer, not lager as now and there was no wine. A woman might have sherry or a port, but I don't remember serving wine. Now they drink gallons. Dad sold his beer cheaper than in other pubs. He'd be charging ten pence a pint, while the pub next door was selling it at a shilling.

Barbara Harrison, born 1937

Mushrooms

Until the war came and we were evacuated to Shropshire, I did not know much about mushrooms. I thought they were things that fairies hid under. One morning the lady with whom we were staying said I could go mushrooming with her. I have never forgotten my first sight of mushrooms growing in a field. They were the large field type and when we had gathered them we took them home. She gave them a wipe and put them in a frying pan with some bacon. I did not fancy the idea but once I tasted those mushrooms, I was hooked. I've loved them ever since.

Elizabeth Edwards, born 1929

Margaret Waddington and Edna Fraser, as bridesmaids in 1951.

Twenty-year-old Barbara Phythian poses in Eastham Woods.

Chinatown

Chinese restaurants started up in Liverpool about forty or fifty years ago. There are a lot now but at first there were only two, in Pitt Street, which was Chinatown.

Elizabeth Li, born 1912

Far East

Liverpool had many wonderful Chinese restaurants when I was young. But the one I remember best was called the Far East. It was quite up-market and housed in a beautiful building, in Chinatown.

Barbara Phythian, born 1929

Chopsticks

Because we were Chinese we lived on Chinese food. We could use chopsticks before we knew how to use a knife and fork. Dad used to do the cooking when our laundry closed at 6.30 p.m. We had one English dinner a week, on a Friday night. A roast.

Susan Grainger, born 1948

Soup

My mother made the most wonderful barley soup, ribs with cabbage. When we went to Fine Fare in London Road, it seemed strange at first because it was so large. Not a bit like the corner shop.

Catherine Riley, born 1960

Reeces

Reeces was very posh in the '50s and '60s. You would go for afternoon tea. Downstairs they had pre-theatre suppers. The menu always seemed to be something and chips. Then, a new place called The Crocodile opened. It was here I had my first taste of scampi. The scampi was wrapped in bacon and served with sauté potatoes.
It was quite a trendy place. We drank gin and orange. Later we graduated to a whisky.

Ann Williams, born 1939

School Dinners

School dinners were horrible when I was growing up on the '40s and early '50s. I suppose it was because my mother was a good cook. The real meal of the week was what today, you would call a mincemeat plate pie. When you were still at school you got a piece of the pie, but when you started work you got your own individual pie in a pie dish. Then you knew you were grown up. My mum made pies of all sorts:, jam pies, damson pies with custard. But you could not keep anything. We could not afford a fridge, so you ate the food at once.

We had cockroaches. You could open a jar of jam and find it full of cockroaches.

We were taught manners as a family but not table manners, something which my wife and I have insisted on in our own children. When you went out into the big wide world, and say, the canteen at work, you'd see all these different knives and forks. I always ate last, to see what people picked up first. And I always ate slowly.

Jim Wafer, born 1944

Plenty

Food was never a problem in our house because even when rationing was on, there were spivs coming in and out of my dad's pub, offering things like tins of salmon. People had the idea that spivs had moustaches and wore long coats, but to me they looked like anyone else. Rationing was still on when I married in 1953 but we had the most wonderful wedding. A detective who came into the pub got us a ham and a whole tongue. We never asked where it came from. The food went like wildfire. We certainly did not go short.

Mum was one of the first to offer food in a pub. There was a shop opposite where the man used to save her the bits of bacon, left after it had been sliced. For some reason she got the idea of serving butter beans and would put them in a pan, with the bacon and a little bit of chopped onion. She served it with a round of Hovis and people came from far and near for it. At one time she was making four large panfuls a day and charging 6d a portion. A customer called Elsie Waite asked if mum would do her favour and throw a pig's foot into the beans next time. She was made up when she did. But when a pan of beans got knocked over by accident and they went all over the passage, mum decided to give up making it. She started doing cheese and onion sandwiches. I still do the butter bean dish.

Barbara Harrison, born 1937

Food Tasted Better

Food seemed to taste better when I was younger. I don't know why because cabbage is cabbage and cauliflower is cauliflower. My grandmother was a marvellous cook. Christmas was always brilliant. She'd make her own puddings and there would be a great big turkey. Being her eldest grandchild, I was the apple of her eye and I would get a turkey drumstick on my plate. I knew where the bottle of dandelion and burdock was kept.

Gwen and Douglas Rafferty with young Ann Roberts in West Street, c. 1941.

Of course we did not have the exotic foods we have now, or the variety. There was no Eastern influence, hot dogs, pizzas and beefburgers and not a lot of Chinese food. It was more a case of plain, wholesome food – fresh carrots, potatoes and meat. Nan cooked tripe and onions in milk. Suet puddings with syrup on top were wonderful, and no doubt full of calories.

School dinners were not bad. I loved egg and bacon pie, then the posh peope hi-jacked it, and called it quiche. There was fish on a Friday and you always had to eat it all. Sometimes you would trade your dinner ticket and sneak out and buy sweets. Chips tasted good when eaten from the old broadsheet *Echo*, with tons of salt and vinegar. Chips tasted better then, as well.

One of the first times I ate out, was when my grandparents treated me to a meal in the Red Rose Restaurant in Lewis'. There was a pianist playing in the middle of the room. My Nan went to Coopers to buy bacon. Coopers was very posh. I loved the smell of all sorts of things, all mixed up, but mainly coffee.

No-one in the family was a heavy drinker. There was drink around at Christmas but, at that time, wine had not been invented as far as Liverpool was concerned. At eighteen we went to Yates Wine Lodge and drank Ozzie White – ruthless stuff. When I was younger my uncle and aunt (she was the only one allowed to cut my nails) took me to the National Milk Bar, opposite Central Station. You could get fruit cake and orange juice. My aunt and uncle had a tandem and used to cycle to Ainsdale.

Michael Penn, born 1945

CHAPTER 7
Into the new millennium

Paul Robeson addresses a meeting at Liverpool's Adelphi in the 1940s. He had been refused a room to stay overnight.

The Halsall girls; Martha, Ann and Mary, c. 1914.

New Century

I cannot see that life is going to alter that much in the twenty-first century. There will still be family groups, people who love each other. We are going to be more integrated with Europe and I am glad about that because we need to stop being so insular. Personally, I want to do more travelling. I have still to get to America, where I want to see the mountains and would also like to go to Australia. Travelling helps you to understand other nations and as I get older, I do try to be more understanding generally.

Diana Dawson, born 1939

IVF

In the medical world, IVF is now a fact of life but I am all mixed up about it myself. It has always been my view that we have no right to interfere with nature. But my niece, who longed for a baby, now has a beautiful little boy.

Ruth Halsall, born 1928

Grandmothers

The family unit is just about hanging on. Family life used to be around the hearth, because then there was not much to hang onto. Your grandmother never went into a home; she lived with you.

Agnes Maddison, born 1927

Grandparents

All today's children want to do is to stay over at these pyjama parties. As a mum and grandmother how do you hold back from saying something that is going to make you an alien? I do talk to them; tell them I've been there and I know where they are at. Today's children are not able to play out in the street because there are so many social perverts about. We were lucky. We learned about our neighbours; how to judge them. Who was good and who was not so good.

Ann Roberts, born 1937

The Motor Car

You wonder what will happen about motoring. It has caused more change in feeling and respect for the police than anything else you can think of. You get one part of the country screaming the place down about motorists being harassed by the police; the other half saying the police are only doing their job.

Arthur Schmuhl, born 1916

The Millennium

By 2012 every taxi will be wheelchair accessible. Now we at the Royal Association for Disability and Rehabilitation need to work on boats and aeroplanes. Eventually we will have to work on space travel because the minute there are trips to space there will be some doctor, saying this is bad for your health and disabled people cannot do it. We'll be there saying 'No, sunshine. If you can go into space, we are going as well.' We do have rights. We are full members of society.

Herbert Massie, born 1949

The Disappearing Years

Between fifty and seventy, you do not know where the years go. It's not so much dying, its the deterioration before death.

Agnes Maddison, born 1927

Alone

When you are on your own and you go to bed at night, you ask yourself 'Is this it?'

Yvonne Puran, born 1964

Vocation

As far as nursing is concerned there is still a strong vocational spirit around. I'd like to see more emphasis on practical skills in the future. There has been too much emphasis on the way nurses are trained. England and its nursing tradition has been looked up to by rest of the world but we have lost it. Thank God I was off the wards before overtime pay came in.

Ruth Halsall, born 1928

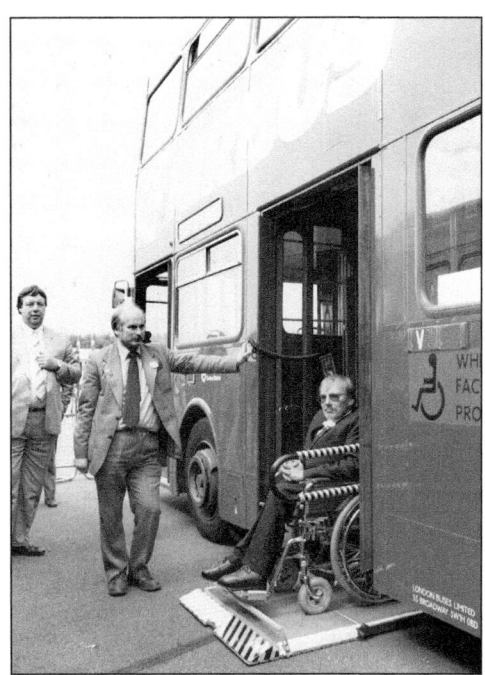

Herbert Massey about to board a wheelchair friendly bus, 1985.

Catholic Church

I do not think the Catholic Church will flourish in the future. People think for themselves now.

Agnes Maddison, born 1927

Black Judges

A lot more women started coming to the Bar in the 1970s and more black people are coming through and taking silk and will become judges. But it takes time and will not happen overnight.

William Wickham, born 1926

Homes

I am fifty-one and fifty-five is the age most people retire from my job. I would have to find another job. My daughter wants to go to university. The thought of going into a home frightens me. I would like to leave my daughter something. I have an insurance policy which covers the cost of the funeral. But I am not covered for residential care.

Tom Eccleston, born 1948

Values

Life has been a great experience. I have no regrets. The way we have lived has given us better values.

Gerry Lipson, born 1929

Gerry Lipson with Ken Dodd at fund raising event for Harold House.

Old People

All my five children are established in good jobs but I wonder what will happen to our grandchildren. When you see old people in homes, they seem to be left to sit there. In that sort of situation, people can deteriorate quite rapidly.

John Griffin, born 1931

Sheltered Accommodation

As people grow older they should have a nice place to live. We are still living the area where we were born, in sheltered accommodation. It is a lovely place. We are happy.

Jack Lindo, born 1919

Young People

I am dreadfully sorry for young people today, in a society with drugs and Aids. I cannot see a way out of it. As far as marriage is concerned, if you marry within your own religion there is a better chance of happiness. Had I wanted to marry a Gentile my father would have gone round the bend. Gone into Shiva which means going into mourning.

David Solomon, born 1916

Trappings

In court you need some trappings. I am in favour of keeping robes in the future. I don't have strong views about wigs. I think eventually they will go. But I think robes should stay: they give a certain solemnity to the occasion.

William Wickham, born 1926

Respect

The public do not have the respect for the police they had. But there has been a big change in policing. The main thing is money. They are up to the eyes in the financial aspects of running a police force. In my day in the force it was not so. I have lived in my present house for twenty years and seen a constable on foot about ten times. Some serious crimes do not seem to get treated seriously. The prisons are so full there is no room to put people in.

Arthur Schmuhl, born 1916

Teaching

Twenty-four years ago when I started teaching in the school where I am now, there was a lot of respect for the profession. Now you feel it is a constant battle and it comes from the home. The children are not as disciplined as when I was a child.

As early as the summer holidays, children are making out lists for their parents telling them what make of clothes they want at Christmas.

Susan Grainger, born 1948

William Wickham with his family, outside the House of Lords, on becoming a Circuit Judge, 1975.

Television

I have strong views on television in court. The Louise Woodward case must have put off televising proceedings for a generation.

William Wickham, born 1926

Pride

Lets hope Liverpool prospers. I have always been proud of my city and hope to go on feeling the same.

Doris Windsor, born 1917

Crime

Crime has changed and will, I suppose, go on changing. It is much more drugs driven now. There are a lot more burglaries and theft caused by demands for drugs. Possession of drugs takes up a lot of time in court today. But other things have altered. Years ago there were a lot of bastardy cases.

William Wickham, born 1926

A Joke

When you go to other parts of the country they laugh at Liverpool. It's a big joke because of Militant and strikes. Just like Arthur Scargill ruined the coal mines, the union leaders ruined the Liverpool docks. The ports on the south-east coast are absolutely thriving, whereas Liverpool's trade has gone. Who knows what the future holds.

Arthur Schmuhl, born 1916

Home

The feeling of belonging will be just as important in the future as it is now. For instance, though we have lived in Southport, quite a while I still feel that Liverpool is home – where our roots are.

Anne Williams, born 1939

Coat Off

Liverpool people will be just as ready to fight for what they want as they have in the past. The Eldonian Village which was established so that people could still live in the inner city if they wished is a good example. As to what the future holds for it, I always tell people, I have not taken my coat off yet.

Tony McGann, born 1937

Hong Kong

When my husband died I took his ashes back to Hongkong. I am not religious but I believe in God. I carried them in a tin, on the plane, and the Customs Officer asked me what I had in it. It was the first time I had met his family; we got on well. I put his ashes on the family grave. They want to know if I want to have my ashes put there as well.

Elizabeth Li, born 1912

Joy and Peace

I do not fear death. I feel then, that I will be able to know what God is, without the obstacles of this life. As it says in the Bible 'I go to prepare a place for you.' I feel I will be going to a place which is full of light and joy and peace.

Lena Prince, born 1923

Money

People will still want to make money in the future. It has been happening since Roman times and before that. As we turn towards the Millennium I am sure British tradition will continue to be thoroughly acceptable in the world. The idea that stockbrokers are all elderly gents, who turn up for three hours and enjoy all the trappings of a rich life, is thirty to forty years out of date. It is an industry, whether in London or the provinces, where you need to work hard and put as much into your professional life as you can. The recession of the '80s and the '90s really pulled people up sharp.

It is interesting that Ford at Halewood have been given the job of building the new Jaguar. Not long ago Halewood was rumoured to be the plant they would like to close down. This is a terrific success story for the region which has possibly has not been trumpeted loud enough.

David Owen, born 1966

Schools

With two small sons, my wife and I will have to consider their education, eventually.

Though I did not have it myself, we might think of educating them privately because I feel that the more children there are in a classroom, the less the child can achieve. On the other hand a state education is equally valid. The privileges which used to be enjoyed from a public school education would appear to be diminished.

As a stockbroker, the industry that I am in now is a meritocracy. It does not really matter which school you went to. Thirty years ago, the school where you were educated would be far more important than your ability.

David Owen, born 1966

Speke

Much as I love it. I do not want to spend the rest of my life in Speke. I want out. I went to live there in 1972, when I was eight, but it did not have the reputation that it does now. There are a lot of changes from when I was growing up. When we were kids we practically lived at the adventure playground. There was nothing much there. It was made of logs and tyres. There is a lot of security in shops in Speke now. Children are not allowed to go in without their parents. Looking to the future, it is no good lining roads with trees. They should put more into houses. As for the kids in the next century, I hope they will all get jobs.

Amanda Brown, born 1964

Tony McGann opens the Eldonian Garden Market.

Fifty Years On

In the next century, I would think, even fifty years hence, we will not recognise different aspects of our everyday life, which we now take for granted. There is a danger that we will become more like America. I hope there is neither the political and moral will to allow that to happen, because to me, it would make this not a particularly nice place to live.

There are certainly too many cars. I would like to see some sort of long tern integrated transport policy in this little island of ours. Otherwise we will all be grid-locked and less healthy because of the air we are breathing.

David Owen, born 1966

Farming

It will be interesting to see what will happen to farming in the next century. We have been through bad times but also moved on from old practices. In 1943 when I took over my farm in Cheshire, I was one of the first in the area to put in a milking machine. We bought our first tractor in 1945. We grew corn during the war because it was compulsory. The foot and mouth outbreak in 1967 was awful. You'd get on the phone to find which farms were affected. Cheshire was badly hit but I was fortunate, we did not get it.

Farmers have always had to diversify. As a child I remember people coming from Liverpool to stay. We had to sleep three in a bed to make room for them. I suppose it was a sort of bed and breakfast, even then. There is nothing new about organic farming. At the beginning of the twentieth century, people had no alternative. Until the Milk Marketing Board came in, the milk business was in a terrible state. We shall see what the future has in store.

Joseph Wilson, born 1914

Shops

It is sad that all the old, well known shops for which Liverpool was famous, are gone. One remembers Frisby Dyke, Philip, Son and Nephew, Cripps in Bold Street, Creamers, the furriers, Russells the watchmakers. They were wonderful places but they all went to the wall. What has taken their place? Modern shops with strobe lighting. But in the end, you must not have regrets about life or what has happened. The future beckons for the young.

David Solomon, born 1916

Early Retirement

Next century, it would be a good thing if people retired earlier and let young people have their jobs. But there are other things which should alter as well. I do not like this single parent thing. It is not good for children and I would like marriage and family life to feature more prominently. There will, I am sure, be even more foreign food eaten. Women will continue to be more equal. The days when the man was expected to be the breadwinner have gone.

Barbara Harrison, born 1937

Technology

The thing about life is that things come back. So we may not see too many changes in the Millennium. My view is that folk will rebel against technology because we need contact with real people. Technology is important but we should make sure we use it and that it does not use us.

Michael Penn, born 1945

Marriage

Marriage is on the way out. I do not see much future for it. What it did was put women into a sort of bondage and they do not need that anymore. I have seen an awful lot of unhappy marriages in my time. Anyway, young people seem to be able to manage their relationships very well, without marriage. Nor do I see much future for religion. When I was a little girl you went to Sunday school automatically. But that has altered. Sunday is now such a precious day that families want to go out and spend it together. There will still be a class system, but again it will be different. It's not just a case of the well off, who have no money worries. knowing their rights. The working class now know them as well.

Jane Saxby, born 1904

Single Parents

Whether the single parent trend will continue, I do not know. I hope not. Every child is entitled to a proper parental background. Then there is the problem of violence, I hope someone sorts that out. It would be nice to go back to the days when the only noise you heard was a kid kicking a can about in the street.

Madge Parry, born 1899

Liverpool Resurgent

We are now seeing business coming back to Liverpool. One of my big bug bears has been the image Liverpool has outside, compared to actually living and working here. We are finally recuperating some of the benefits of a change in people's perception of the city and what it is like to do business here. What has happened is that the speciality and investment that has been gleaned over decades has ensured that there is a thriving community of firms, managing money, out of Liverpool.

People ask me why I have not left. It is because apart from the fact that I am Northern boy at heart – and a home boy – I believe in the area. A lot of my friends live and work in London, but it has never appealed to me. I shall retire in my mid-fifties. I don't want to go on until I am sixty-five. Life is here for the living, rather than being a wage slave.

The main thing I have missed out on is seeing the world. I would like to see more of it.

David Owen, born 1966